RESPONDING TO INTIMATE VIOLENCE AGAINST WOMEN

Family members, friends, co-workers, and neighbors are often the first to know that a woman has been abused by an intimate male partner. What is the proper course of action for those with knowledge of abuse? Using a wide range of empirical data from international sources, Renate Klein documents informal third parties as the first port of call, sources of support and interference, and gatekeepers to formal services. Family and social network members disrupt ongoing assaults, respond to disclosures of abuse, and provide solace and practical help. These networks do not always side with victims, however, and may either sympathize with or actively support perpetrators.

Klein illuminates the complexities of these contingent situations. Her analysis highlights the potential of informal third parties for effective intervention, demonstrating their significant role in promoting societies free from rape and domestic violence.

Renate Klein grew up in Germany and studied psychology at the University of Marburg. Since relocating to the United States in the 1990s, Klein has collaborated with international partners on projects related to gender, culture, violence, and violence prevention. She initiated an interdisciplinary network of researchers addressing gender and violence in Europe, which has fostered international collaborations and serves as a forum for constructive debate in this field. Klein has also supported voluntary sector-led research in the United States and England, working as a research consultant for nonprofit organizations in central Maine.

Advances in Personal Relationships

Series Editors

Anita L. Vangelisti
University of Texas, Austin

Christopher R. Agnew
Purdue University

John P. Caughlin
University of Illinois at Urbana-Champaign

Susan Sprecher
Illinois State University

Although scholars from a variety of disciplines have written and conversed about the importance of personal relationships for decades, the emergence of personal relationships as a field of study is relatively recent. *Advances in Personal Relationships* represents the culmination of years of multidisciplinary and interdisciplinary work on personal relationships. Sponsored by the International Association for Relationship Research, the series offers readers cutting-edge research and theory in the field. Contributing authors are internationally known scholars from a variety of disciplines, including social psychology, clinical psychology, communication, history, sociology, gerontology, and family studies. Volumes include integrative reviews, conceptual pieces, summaries of research programs, and major theoretical works. *Advances in Personal Relationships* presents first-rate scholarship that is both provocative and theoretically grounded. The theoretical and empirical work described by authors will stimulate readers and advance the field by offering new ideas and retooling old ones. The series will be of interest to upper division undergraduate students, graduate students, researchers, and practitioners.

Other Books in the Series

Attribution, Communication Behavior, and Close Relationships
Valerie Manusov and John H. Harvey, editors

Stability and Change in Relationships
Anita L. Vangelisti, Harry T. Reis, and Mary Anne Fitzpatrick, editors

Understanding Marriage: Developments in the Study of Couple Interaction
Patricia Noller and Judith A. Feeney, editors

Growing Together: Personal Relationships Across the Life Span
Frieder R. Lang and Karen L. Fingerman

Communicating Social Support
Daena J. Goldsmith

Communicating Affection: Interpersonal Behavior and Social Context
Kory Floyd

Changing Relations: Achieving Intimacy in a Time of Social Transition
Robin Goodwin

Feeling Hurt in Close Relationships
Anita L. Vangelisti, editor

Responding to Intimate Violence Against Women

The Role of Informal Networks

Renate Klein

University of Maine and
London Metropolitan University

CAMBRIDGE
UNIVERSITY PRESS

CAMBRIDGE UNIVERSITY PRESS
Cambridge, New York, Melbourne, Madrid, Cape Town,
Singapore, São Paulo, Delhi, Mexico City

Cambridge University Press
32 Avenue of the Americas, New York, NY 10013-2473, USA

www.cambridge.org
Information on this title: www.cambridge.org/9780521849852

First published 2012

Printed in the United States of America

A catalog record for this publication is available from the British Library.

Library of Congress Cataloging in Publication Data

Klein, Renate, 1959–
Responding to intimate violence against women : the role of informal networks / Renate Klein.
p. cm. – (Advances in personal relationships)
Includes bibliographical references and index.
ISBN 978-0-521-84985-2
1. Women – Crimes against – Prevention. 2. Women – Social networks. I. Title.
HV6250.4.W65K585 2012
362.82′92–dc23 2012017430

ISBN 978-0-521-84985-2 Hardback

CONTENTS

1

Introduction

This book is about the role of family members, friends, and co-workers in sexual and domestic violence against women. Informal third parties often are aware of abuse because they have witnessed an abusive episode, heard about it from the victim, or know what the perpetrator did. They may not know the full extent of what is going on, but they often know something. In a surprising number of cases, there are witnesses. Every time a victim tells somebody about abuse, another person beyond victim and perpetrator knows. What do we do with this knowledge?

Sometimes we do nothing, thinking we can remain neutral: "One white woman said, 'Friends came around and saw from the beginning. He smacked me in front of them, saying 'Oh shut up, you're getting on my nerves.' They got up and walked out saying they can't get involved'" (Hanmer, 2000, p. 15). Sometimes we are silent, although we know what is going on: "His uncle abuses his aunt and everybody in his family can tell, but they never say a word about it" (Bancroft, 2002, p. 276). Sometimes we intervene: "Wolk, 46, was arrested after five female Husson students subdued him following the knife attack on his then-wife of seven years" (*Bangor Daily News*, October 5, 2011). "'There was already another girl there, and she was kind of behind him trying to do something . . . as

I went to grab the guy's hand, I saw he had a nice little knife in his hand . . . A couple of other girls joined us and we just got him down on the ground until security came" (*Bangor Daily News*, May 5, 2010). Often we doubt her story: "I live with my husband's parents and brother. Whatever my husband tells my mother-in-law, all the blame falls on me" (Menjívar & Salcido, 2002, p. 904).

Knowledge of abuse among family, friends, or co-workers is awareness of the problem close to home, not merely as a distant social issue. This makes it particularly challenging, but it also opens windows of opportunity because informal third parties are a potential, and largely untapped, resource for intervention, prevention, and social change. The purpose of this book is to review research on informal responses and explore the interpersonal dynamics surrounding sexual and domestic violence against women who are close to us as sisters, daughters, mothers, friends, co-workers, or neighbors. The goal is to offer a third-party perspective on the social dynamics in which such abuse unfolds and in which it may be prevented.

In this introductory chapter, several issues are addressed to set the stage for the exploration of informal responses. This includes clarifying the context and purpose of the book and delineating its thematic scope. After that, the significance of informal third parties as a first port of call will be highlighted. This chapter concludes with comments on terminology used in the book and previews of the following chapters.

CONTEXT AND PURPOSE

Informal third parties are often the first to know if somebody close to them is abused. In many cases, police or victim-support services never become involved; informal third parties then are the only ones who know and the only potential source of support (Hanmer, 2000; Hoff, 1990; Kelly, 1996). Informal third parties respond in different ways: by offering and refusing help, blaming victims, excusing perpetrators, disrupting assaults, dismissing the seriousness of abuse, consoling victims, or taking revenge on perpetrators. Network members may provide emotional and material support, shelter, transportation, money, or childcare; a Canadian survey found that three-fourths of women who left an abusive partner stayed with friends or family during the process of leaving (Rodgers, 1994). Of 158 U.S. women who were survivors of intimate partner abuse and whose cases had reached the courts, all said that a third party knew of the abuse (Belknap et al., 2009). Most common among the third parties were relatives and friends, including the women's children and members of the perpetrator's family, followed by neighbors, co-workers, or classmates. Additional third parties included landlords, teachers, and the children's day care staff.

Some informal responses are helpful and some are not; many victims experience a mix of both. Hanmer (2000) found that friends and family responded to abuse in

> contradictory ways. The responses of others are frequently characterized by alternating behaviours as support moves between the woman and the man. Thus a son may be told to stop hitting his wife when directly observed, to which he may or may not respond, while his parents may demand that [the victim] apologize for upsetting [the perpetrator] when she has been badly beaten on another occasion, but it has not been seen by them. Interventions may be ambiguous and erratic, as family members are pulled this way and that by competing and contradictory values, views and feelings. (p. 14)
>
> When confronted with repeated violence, women describe how family members and others intervene in women's lives and how women attempt to use networks of family and friends to mitigate, if not resolve, problems with their men. (p. 10)

Research attention paid to informal third parties has ebbed and flowed since the early days of the field. After a trickle of studies in the 1970s and 1980s in the United Kingdom and North America, research activity increased in the 1990s and the 2000s (Binney, Harkell, & Nixon, 1981; Prescott & Letko, 1977; Tan et al., 1995; Ullman, 2010). Interest in informal responses has grown, perhaps in part because of the hope that they will aid early intervention and prevention of abuse (see Budde & Scheune, 2004, with regard to informal interventions in child abuse). However, research on informal responses remains fragmented in several ways.

Informal responses are an important social phenomenon but not an integrated field of research. Lines of inquiry are scattered across separate bodies of literature; there is no single theory or conceptual framework. Data are collected with different methods to answer specific research questions without necessarily integrating findings theoretically; studies that could complement each other are often not considered in conjunction. Most studies have focused on informal responses to victims, whereas comparatively few have considered responses to perpetrators. As a result, the interpersonal dynamics in the social networks of perpetrators are not systematically integrated into understandings of the social context at large, although social ties often connect victims and perpetrators within the same familial, social, or work-related networks (DeKeseredy, 1990; Raghavan et al., 2009). Furthermore, relatively little attention has been paid to the body of anthropological work about gender dynamics in societies in which rape and domestic violence are rare, although this research illustrates not only the existence of shared worldviews incompatible with abuse but also the third-party actions that put these worldviews into practice in everyday life (Counts, Brown, & Campbell, 1999; Lepowsky, 1993; McGillivray & Comaskey, 1999; Watson-Franke, 2002).

At present, there is an intriguing, yet fragmented, body of evidence on informal third parties that deserves a closer, more integrated analysis. To overcome this fragmentation, evidence of informal responses from different lines of research is gathered here in one place in order to present an overview of current knowledge and explore implications for research and practice. One goal in this book is to highlight links among lines of inquiries, in particular between responses to victims and responses to perpetrators. For instance, blaming the victim implies shifting blame away from the perpetrator; doing nothing often means giving the perpetrator free reign. Informal responses vary and are often contradictory, and, for the most part, the uptake of such findings in wider intervention debates is still in its early stages. This has hampered an examination of the concurrent impact of informal responses on victims and perpetrators, the interplay of informal responses and formal interventions, and their net effects on victim well-being.

Another goal is to examine the potential of informal responses for intervention and long-term prevention of abuse. As a whole, relationships with family, friends, co-workers, and neighbors constitute significant social sites for both enabling and thwarting abuse; the quality of third-party responses shapes contexts that are more or less conducive or resistant to abuse. In this sense, "domestic violence . . . is bred of many interactions, not just the one that transpires between the person who inflicts injury and the one who sustains it" (Baumgartner, 1993, p. 228). The importance of informal third parties begins with the presence of third parties during episodes of abuse and continues with their role as first port of call, which in turn shapes trajectories of healing, recovery, and redress. Informal third parties, in different ways, are positioned toward the conduits of power and influence in families, communities, and workplaces and may be able to marshal emotional, symbolic, and material resources from which victims or perpetrators can benefit.

To address these issues, diverse informal third-party actions are examined in conjunction. It is hoped that the reader will gain a better understanding of their breadth, variety, and combined impact on both victims and perpetrators. Ideally, this will contribute to knowledge based on a critical appreciation of empirical evidence, confident of the evidence's ability to reflect real, lived experience, yet mindful that what we see reflected in research also depends on the conceptual frameworks used to interpret data.

The book is directed at advanced students in the social and health sciences, but it may also be of interest for professionals in these fields and others who are interested in a fresh perspective on the social context of abuse and its prevention. The primary reason for writing it was recognition that informal third parties are more important to intervention than they have been given credit for. This refers to their role in supporting victims and to their equally important but more problematic role in siding with perpetrators. Although there now is considerable evidence on informal responses, on the whole they have remained in the shadow of other topics of research. Most of the research examined here is from Anglo-Saxon countries, in particular the United States, the United Kingdom, and Canada, but research from other countries is included as well. No formal framework for cross-national comparison is used, but the evidence suggests that informal responses are an important issue in many different countries.

THEMATIC SCOPE

Most of the empirical studies considered in this book focus on informal responses to sexual and domestic violence against women of childbearing age perpetrated by men in the context of sexual or family relationships (Holder, 1998; Kelly, 1996; Ullman, 2010). This research documented a range of informal third-party actions including the responses of witnesses to ongoing or imminent assaults (see Chapter 4), responses to victims' disclosure and help-seeking (Chapter 5), and responses to, or relationships with, perpetrators (Chapter 6). This empirical material spans four decades of research from 1977 to 2011. Also included is some of the ethnographic research in societies in which rape and domestic violence appear to be extremely rare.

Informal responses are likely to also matter in relation to other patterns of abuse including abuse in gay and lesbian relationships (Bornstein et al., 2006; Oringher & Samuelson, 2011), rape of men by other men (Vearnals & Campbell, 2001), abuses in institutions (Gasch, 2010), and child sexual abuse (Arata, 1998; Bottoms, Rudnicki, & Epstein, 2007). However, the social and institutional contexts in which these patterns of abuse occur vary considerably, including the role of age differences and homophobia, and although there may be similarities across contexts, the present discussion focuses primarily on informal responses to sexual and domestic abuse against women of childbearing age in heterosexual relationships. There are several reasons for this focus.

Women of childbearing age are the population group worldwide most at risk for sexual and domestic abuse (Reed et al., 2010). They and their children suffer most of the health consequences of domestic violence, ranging from injury, stress-related trauma, and chronic disease to reproductive health problems and poor child health (Ellsberg et al., 2008; Martinez et al. 2006). In addition, quite a lot is known about the range of social contexts in which sexual and domestic abuses occur and the compounding effects of poverty and racism (Goodman et al., 2009; Sokoloff & Pratt, 2005). There also is evidence, ironically, of sociocultural contexts in which the rape and beating of women appear to be rare or nonexistent (Counts et al., 1999; Watson-Franke, 2002). Finally, *formal* interventions in rape and domestic violence against women are relatively well developed, in particular with regard to victim-support services and criminal justice measures (Hanmer et al., 2006; Hester & Westmarland, 2005; Humphreys et al., 2006; Sullivan, 2005). Thus, there are best-practice frameworks for service delivery and other formal interventions that can put the prevention potential of informal responses into perspective.

INFORMAL THIRD PARTIES AS A FIRST PORT OF CALL

Empirical studies routinely find that most victims turn to social network members first, and most never engage formal services. Informal third parties are often the first and, in many cases, the only people who know of abuse, which makes the quality of their responses particularly important for the further course of recovery and redress. When formal third parties do not become involved at all, informal responses are the only potential source of support and intervention.

In the United States, Fisher et al. (2003) found that female college students disclosed sexual assault mostly to informal third parties. Only 2% of victims reported sexual violence to police, 4% reported it to campus authorities, and yet 70% told somebody else. Of those who told somebody else, 88% told a friend, 10% a family member, and 8% an intimate (1% told counseling services; percentages exceed 100 because multiple responses were possible). Kaukinen and DeMaris (2009) conducted a reanalysis of the National Survey on Violence Against Women in the United States and found that 73% asked family, friends, or neighbors for help; 27% reported the assault to police.

In Britain, early studies had shown that women who were experiencing domestic violence approached family and friends, in particular mothers, about three times as often as they approached formal systems such as the police (Kelly, 1996). More recently, Povey et al. (2009) also found that more victims of sexual or domestic violence report to informal third parties than to police. In the 2009–10 British Crime Survey, 38% of victims of serious sexual assault told no one about it; 62% told someone (Smith et al., 2011). Whom did they tell? Victims most often confided in friends, relatives, or neighbors: 45% of those victims who disclosed at all (or 28% of all victims surveyed); 11% of those who told anyone reported the assault to police (or 7% of all victims surveyed; 93% of assaults were not reported to police) (Smith et al., 2011).

Only a few women who experience abuse find their way to support services or formal authorities. For the United States, Kilpatrick, Edmunds, and Seymour (1992) found that 16% of victims told police; 26% told a doctor. Low reporting rates were also found more recently: In a national sample of women, 16% of rapes were reported to police; in a sample of college women, 12% of rapes were reported to police (Kilpatrick et al., 2007). Reasons for not reporting to police included not wanting others to know, lack of proof, fear of reprisal by perpetrator, and fear of secondary victimization through the criminal justice system (Fisher et al., 2003). Suspicion of the criminal justice system is another reason not to report, in particular where law enforcement is seen as racist and ineffective (Hamby, 2008).

Other studies found that rape victims are least likely to disclose to formal providers including police, physicians, and rape crisis centers (Ahrens & Campbell, 2000; Ullman, 1996, 2000). In a study of rape survivors who had disclosed the rape, three-quarters of the first confidantes were informal third parties (Ahrens et al., 2007). Survivors most commonly told a friend (38.2%) or a family member (22.5%); and less often they told their partners (5.9%), a co-worker (3.9%), a neighbor (3.9%), or a stranger (2.9%). Only 15% of first disclosures were to formal third parties such as police (5.9%), doctor (4.9%), therapist (2.9%), or clergy (1.0). Slightly less than 10% of the women told no one (which makes this study one of several in which disclosure in the context of research was the first time the victim told anybody. For some victims the first-ever disclosure is in research; reasons are guilt, shame, and fear of not being believed, especially if a boyfriend is the rapist) (Ullman, 2010).

If women survivors seek support from specialized services such as rape crisis centers or domestic violence projects, they typically are very satisfied with the support they receive, but only a small percentage of women access these services. One basic problem still is that, even though excellent services exist, they tend to cluster in urban areas; for too many victims, specialized services may be too far away (Coy, Kelly, & Foord, 2007). At the same time, access to services and the pathways by which victims reach rape crisis centers or domestic violence projects may also change over time as availability of services, public awareness of them, and referral practices among formal third parties change. In the late 1980s, Golding et al. (1989) found that 1.9% of rape victims had turned to a rape crisis center (16.1% to a mental health professional), but among all formal services, rape crisis centers were most often named as helpful – a dilemma documented repeatedly: The frequent accessing of services does not mean users found them effective or satisfying (Hamilton & Coates, 1993). Around the same time, George, Winfield, and Blazer (1992) reported for two urban United States samples that 5% of sexual assault victims sought help from a rape crisis center, whereas 27% turned to a psychiatrist or mental health counselor. In 2009, Kaukinen and DeMaris reported that 4.7% of sexual assault victims had contacted a social service agency (unspecified) and 9.4% had been referred to specialized victim services by police. The dilemma that few victims can benefit from excellent service may be most pronounced with regard to specialized victim services but can also concern police. Of the victims surveyed in the 2009–10 British Crime Survey who did tell police about a serious sexual assault, the majority found the police to be fairly helpful or very helpful (Smith et al., 2011).

Hence, formal interventions by victim-support services and the criminal justice system are important, but relatively low use limits their effectiveness. For many victims, support services may be out of reach because they are too far away or regarded with suspicion; police are called only in a minority of cases and usually only when an abusive episode has escalated. Health care providers who may see victims of abuse in the context of routine health care do not always have the training to respond appropriately (Allen et al., 2007; Tower et al., 2006).

Considering that survivors are likely to turn to informal third parties if they disclose at all, there should be considerable awareness of abuse among friends and social networks, although the extent to which this is true may vary by population. Where young people live close together, such as college students in North America, a significant number of third parties are likely to know rape survivors. Dunn, Vail-Smith, and Knight (1999) found that 282 out of 828 college students (about one-third) had been told by at least one female friend that she had been raped, and a smaller percentage of students had heard from more than one victim. A few years earlier, Frazier and Burnett (1994) had found that by the third day after a rape, victims, on average, had told about four people about it, finding sisters and rape trauma nurses most supportive and male friends and boyfriends least supportive. Victims had been contacted through a specialized sexual assault resource service in a large city; it is unclear how many of them might have been students or other community members. More recently, Banyard et al. (2010), in a study of undergraduate students at the University of New Hampshire, found that one in three women, and one in five men, had been told by a friend that she had been sexually assaulted. These findings suggest that informal responses should be considered more closely for their potential to deliver social support, connect victims to specialist resources, and realize long-term, sustainable social change.

The importance of social networks for victims of sexual and domestic abuse has been observed in different countries (Fisher et al., 2003; Hoff, 1990; Holder, 1998; Kelly, 1996; Rodgers, 1994). Holder (1998) concluded that

> these studies show, overwhelmingly, the same pattern. Women turn FIRST to friends, family and neighbours. Around 20–30% turn to police. GPs [general practitioners, i.e., primary health care providers] are the next most contacted formal agency, and then a smaller proportion use a range of social and community agencies such as refuges [shelters] . . . the critical feature of all these findings is the reliance women place in seeking help from and through family, friends and neighbours – the community. (pp. 4–5; emphasis in the original)

Because family or network members are often the first to know, their responses are important in shaping the future trajectory of coping and may set the course for recovery, healing, or further distress. Supportive responses can make victims feel better and support coping, whereas negative responses such as silencing, blame, anger, or doing nothing increase victim distress and may undermine their efforts at help-seeking (Ahrens, 2006; Ahrens & Campbell, 2000; Ahrens et al., 2007; Hoff, 1990; Symonds, 1980/2010). In one study, negative informal responses worsened posttraumatic stress after sexual assault (Borja, Callahan, & Long, 2006).

Because informal third parties often are closer (physically, emotionally, or culturally) to victim and perpetrator than formal services, their actions are a significant aspect of intervention and prevention. Nonetheless, there still "is minimal acknowledgement of the extent to which we all know about the existence of violence against women, let alone creation of an enabling culture to address it more constructively" (Kelly & Lovett, 2005, p. 8). It is important to better understand informal responses and their capacity to make a positive difference. By offering or withholding support to victims, leaning on perpetrators, or siding with perpetrators, informal third parties have a role in how difficult it is for victims to seek safety and redress for themselves and their children. An analysis of informal responses, as provided in this book, promises new insights into long-standing debates about gender dynamics, victim impacts, and prevention practice.

NOTES ON TERMINOLOGY

The term *informal third party* is used here to emphasize that there are more than two parties (victim and perpetrator) to consider; abusive actions do not occur in a social vacuum, even if they happen in a physically isolated place (Baumgartner, 1993). Furthermore, family or network members are not passive fixtures in the configuration of social ties, but are interested third parties whose responses to abuse are shaped by their own values, hopes, fears, and loyalties (Klein & Milardo, 1993). Abusive actions occur within social networks, and informal responses are woven into the attachments, loyalties, and obligations these very networks produce (Klein, 2004).

The word *abuse* is used interchangeably with *violence*. Violence carries strong connotations of physical injury, which should be maintained because some abuse is physically violent. However, many actions constitute sexual and emotional abuse or coercive control without being physically violent but are still harmful and damaging. Expressions like sexual and domestic violence against women, intimate abuse of women, rape, and domestic abuse are used interchangeably. The term *victim* is used to refer to those who suffer the bulk of harm from rape and domestic violence, and the term *perpetrator* is used to refer to those who do the harming. This distinction is made regardless of whether victims also physically fight back to defend themselves. Occasionally, victims are referred to as *survivors.* The term victim has been rejected as too passive by many in the field who prefer the term survivor. Victim is used here not to denote passivity or helplessness but to emphasize the contrast between victim and perpetrator and to emphasize that informal responses have implications for both.

The word *social* is understood as synonymous with *cultural* and vice versa. Using social for "us" and cultural for "them" reflects an arbitrary distinction between what is presumed to be "normal" and what is presumed to be "different." The term culture tends to be used to get at some assumed or real essence of a group, "them in a nutshell," so to speak. This easily leads to simplistic, stereotypical portrayals, which have been criticized in debates about violence against women (Sen, 2005), in particular for the sensationalism and implied finger-pointing involved when women are portrayed as victims of "bad cultures" (Narayan, 1997) or when culture is used as an excuse for abuse or a reason not to intervene. One could do without the term culture altogether, but despite its shortcomings, it is useful as shorthand for shared beliefs and taken-for-granted practices, both aspects that are crucial in creating worlds without abuse. In addition, the experience of abuse and the process of coping are likely to be culturally mediated. Deer (2004) argued that Native American women in the United States not only need an "indigenous jurisprudence of rape" (because both tribal justice systems and mainstream U.S. legal responses are inadequate) but also culturally relevant support because their response to abuse is inflected by their cultural identity and history. The latter argument has been made repeatedly and in different countries in regard to the provision of services to minority women who are victims of sexual or domestic violence (Abraham, 2000; Dasgupta, 2007; Gillum, 2009; McGillivray & Comaskey, 1999).

CHAPTER PREVIEWS

Chapter 2 examines third-party responses in societies in which sexual and domestic violence against women appears to be absent or extremely rare. Historical records and anthropological research suggest that several indigenous societies have been able to establish social practices in which sexual and domestic violence has no place. Such practices illustrate in the mundane detail of daily life how third parties can sustain nonviolent gender relations as a normal (normative and widely shared) societal achievement. This evidence also helps us to rethink nonabusive gender relations in the positive: not just as an absence of cruelty, coercion, and exploitation but as a presence of considerate and respectful relating. This is not a matter of everlasting bliss, but of hard interpersonal work to be done anew every day.

Chapter 3 provides a theoretical framework in which to interpret the diverse evidence on informal responses. Inspired by Chapter 2, and aware of the theoretical diversity of the research examined in Chapters 4, 5, and 6, this framework focuses on three societal forces whose interplay appears to be significant for the social construction of women's sexual and domestic authority: social ties, gender beliefs, and the construction of personhood.

Chapter 4 examines preemption and disruption of assaults focusing on children's intervention in domestic violence and on peer dynamics around rape at college parties. Third parties as witnesses who intervene in an assault have received relatively little attention, but startling evidence is available about the role of children in trying to defend their mothers against attacks from male intimates. In relation to peer education at United States colleges, there is growing interest in the role of students as active bystanders to sexual violence who can be taught how to disrupt the buildup to sexual assaults.

Chapter 5 concerns third-party responses to disclosure of abuse and requests for help. Some studies have focused on the disclosure of rape, others on the disclosure of domestic violence. The research examined for this book shows that the quality of third-party responses shapes a victim's pathways toward recovery: Supportive responses encourage healing, whereas unsupportive responses can isolate and traumatize victims further. Responses to help-seeking also vary; some third parties give support, whereas others refuse to become involved. Although most of this research focused on responses to victims, it also uncovered the fact that sometimes informal third parties try to lean on the perpetrator to desist.

Chapter 6 focuses on collusion with perpetrators. Research here includes studies on abusive friends in the social networks of perpetrators, old-boys' networks that link perpetrators to agents of the state, and the shielding of perpetrators by superiors in organizational hierarchies in the workplace.

Chapter 7 provides a summary and conclusions.

2

Lessons from Egalitarian Societies

In his book on the history of nonviolence, Mark Kurlansky notes that major religions have praised the idea of nonviolence, yet

> while every major language has a word for violence, there is no word to express the idea of nonviolence except that it is not another idea, it is not violence. The only possible explanation for the absence of a proactive word to express nonviolence is that not only the political establishments but the cultural and intellectual establishments of all societies have viewed nonviolence as a marginal point of view . . . not an authentic concept but simply the abnegation of something else. It has been marginalized because it is one of the rare truly revolutionary ideas, an idea that seeks to completely change the nature of society, a threat to the established order. (Kurlansky, 2008, p. 5)

Kurlansky focused on political violence and warfare, but his point matters for sexual and domestic abuse as well: Nonabusive gender practices do appear to be a marginal point of view, reflected in a lack of a widely used concept that would capture the essence of what goes on in nonabusive relating. Although prevention of rape and domestic violence ranks high on local, national, and international agendas, nonabuse in gender relations continues to be defined primarily as an absence rather than a presence. Many countries and jurisdictions nowadays have nondiscrimination policies on the books, and programs for young people on how to have healthy and respectful relationships are increasingly common. Yet, in the rhetoric articulating these advancements calls for eliminating abuse are more common than explications of what to put in its place. This absence of positive naming and conceptualization of gendered nonviolence is reflected semantically in the use of negations (nonviolence, nonabuse, nondiscrimination) and in metaphors borrowed from other fields of practice (healthy relationships). Without proper naming, nonabusive gender practices remain invisible.

Although it is important to call for an end to abuse, the pathways toward this goal also need to be thought out and articulated in the positive – as what ought to be present, not merely as what ought to be absent. Feminists have pointed out that the threat and actual perpetration of sexual and domestic abuse are woven into the very nature of gender relations where these exist within patriarchal orders in which femaleness is devalued and men consider themselves entitled to women's sexual and domestic services (Dobash & Dobash, 1979; Martin, 1981). From this perspective, preventing sexual and domestic abuse is not a matter of hoping for kinder patriarchs who will not abuse; it is a matter of changing the social context of gender relations to one in which femaleness is valued, women are fully acknowledged members of society, and patterns of inconsiderate or cruel exploitation of women are preempted or disrupted.

The social context for this sort of social change to take place in includes laws, norms, discourses, and worldviews, but it takes real people in the vicinity of victims and perpetrators to fill abstract societal concepts with significance for lived experience: family and kin, friends and co-workers, neighbors, community leaders, and people in workplaces and institutions. What do they do where sexual and domestic abuse against women is absent or rare?

Ethnographic research is informative in this regard. It offers tantalizing evidence that although societies without rape and wife-beating are rare, they exist, they are real, and they show that nonabuse is a matter of particular socially shared gender practices in which third parties have an important part. Although this research is rarely integrated into mainstream prevention discourses, it converges in surprising ways with findings from ethnographic and psychological research in so-called Western societies. For understanding nonabuse in the positive, gender practices in egalitarian societies offer interesting lessons.

THIRD-PARTY PRACTICES WHERE RAPE AND DOMESTIC VIOLENCE ARE ABSENT OR RARE

The following discussion draws on compilations of ethnographic fieldwork that focused on societies without wife-beating (Counts et al., 1999; Levinson 1989) and societies in which men do not rape women (Watson-Franke, 2002). This material offers the only extant evidence on nonabusive gender practices on a "culture-wide" scale (for lack of a better term) in which nonabusive worldviews and egalitarian structures converge with widely shared considerate gender relations. Although most of the world appears to be steeped in, or to struggle with, the legacies of hierarchical, exploitative gender traditions, these are neither universal nor inevitable. Some societies have managed to do much better.

This evidence comes from different parts of the world and has been compiled over a span of several decades, using diverse methodologies and terminologies. For example, Levinson (1989) did not use terms such as "sexual violence against women and girls," although he lists practices that would constitute such abuses (child marriage, child prostitution, gang rape of girls, marital rape, wife raiding).

The organization of gender in society occurs on multiple levels that are not necessarily consistent with each other and may be contradictory. Lepowsky (1993) noted that "recent discussions of gender theory in anthropology have stressed that cultures or societies do not have one unique, monolithic and noncontradictory ideology of gender operating in the thoughts of each person on all occasions" (p. 34). Under the influence of postmodernism and poststructuralism, ideas about cultures have been recast to allow for more "cultural ambiguities" (p. 34). For instance, the notion of a single social status (for women or men) or of a single-gender ideology has given way to the realization that women can be more or less advantaged on different dimensions and multiple-gender ideologies can coexist (Connell, 2006; Walby, 2004a).

In one attempt to represent the complexity of social status, Wieringa (1997) extracted eight dimensions of gender equality or women's status: gender identity (socialization, gender roles); autonomy of the body (absence of violence against women, control over sexuality and reproduction); autonomy within the household (freedom to marry and divorce, custody rights, within-household decision-making power and access to assets); political power (at above household levels: municipal, unions, government, parliament); social resources (access to health care and education); material resources (access to land, houses, and credit); employment and income (distribution of paid and unpaid work, wage differentials, formal and informal labor); and time (access to leisure and sleep is gendered with a gender gap in amount of "free time"; see Mattingly and Bianchi, 2003, for an analysis of U.S. data).

Gender equality indices such as the Gender-Related Development Index (GDI) and the Gender Empowerment Measure (GEM), both developed within the United Nations Development Program, tended to focus on outcomes such as educational attainment, life expectancy, income, or share in parliament. Such indicators measure absolute levels of achievement rather than gender equality as such and say little about the social practices underlying such achievements (Dijkstra, 2002). In an effort to construct more meaningful equality indicators, the Organization for Economic Cooperation and Development launched a Social Institutions and Gender Index (SIGI) that focuses less on gendered outcomes and more on the institutions and practices likely to produce such outcomes (even though some of the new categories, such as physical integrity, could be considered outcomes) (Organization for Economic Cooperation and Development, 2009). Of additional concern here is the problem that indices of gender equality may bear no clear relation to women's risk of sexual or domestic violence, as subsequently illustrated.

Similar to complexities of social status, gender ideologies are often complex and contradictory so that "general" gender ideologies or norms can coexist with contradictory, more specific "gender meanings" (Schlegel, 1990). For example, the general norm that it is unmanly to hit a woman coexists with more specific beliefs expressed in rape myths (Burt, 1980) and domestic violence myths (Peters, 2008) that under certain circumstances men could or should rape and hit women.

Lepowsky also noted that the presence of such ideological contradictions and ambiguities may be more common in societies in which gender equality in theory coexists with gender inequality in practice. There seems to be less ambiguity the other way round: Where gender equality is practiced in everyday life, including intimate heterosexual relationships, gender norms seem to reflect rather than disguise actual practice. Among the Vanatinai, Lepowsky observed that abstract gender principles, specific meanings, and daily practice were quite consistent, which led her to conclude that "this ideological congruence is a highly significant feature of cultures with a strong tendency toward gender equality" (1993, p. 35).

The relationship among norms, social structures, and gender practices is of interest in studies that have tried to relate differences in prevalence of sexual and domestic violence to differences in sociocultural contexts. In a comparative study of ninety societies, Levinson (1989) tried to identify social status indicators that correlate with wife-beating. He coded the frequency of wife-beating into several categories: rare or absent; infrequent, occurs in 49% or less of households; frequent, occurs in more than 50% of households; and common, occurs in all or nearly all households. Wife-beating was more frequent where men had control over the distribution of monetary or material products of the labor of household members, where men had final say in domestic decision making, where a deceased husband's kin controlled whom his widow could marry, and where men could take multiple wives and could divorce more easily than women.

Wife-beating was absent or rare in societies in which women had control over the fruits of their labor and influence over household decisions, in which women had a degree of sexual autonomy (that is, where they were able to decide whom to marry and where they could get a divorce), and in which women could form coalitions and rally allies outside of family networks (such as all-female work groups). Just as notable, responsibility for the care of boys and the location of postmarital residence were not significantly correlated with frequency of wife-beating.

Levinson (1989) found that the immediate statistical predictors of wife-beating were men's domestic authority (their final say in family decision making) and women's lack of divorce options. Both, in turn, were influenced by economic inequality, with control of family output having the strongest association with domestic authority. Levinson concluded that, in a cross-cultural perspective, "male control of wealth and property is the basic cause of wife beating" (1989, p. 73). Basic cause here does not suggest a quasi-mechanical process that makes wife-beating happen. Instead, the societal arrangements Levinson described increase the likelihood of wife-beating because they put husbands in a powerful position over wives and undermine safeguards that could protect wives against individual husbands' abuse of such power.

Levinson (1989) also found that infanticide sex preference was not correlated with wife-beating, suggesting that different forms of gender-based violence may not be correlated with each other and that what protects against one form may not protect against another. This could mean, for instance, that even if wife-beating were to end, other forms of abuse might continue, including abortion of girl fetuses or neglect or killing of girls, sexual violence, or nonphysical coercion. This also suggests that intervention and prevention efforts focused on ending specific acts of violence or narrowly defined patters of abuse (such as physical violence) may have no or little effect on other forms of abuse (such as coercion, exploitation, or rape).

The findings also caution against assuming simple relationships between gender equality and prevention of violence against women. Legal and economic reforms designed to reduce domestic violence (for instance, by making it easier for women to separate from abusive husbands or partners) may not affect abuses that are less predicated on women being trapped in a relationship with an abusive man (such as abuse in dating relationships that may be easier to dissolve than a marriage or rape in the context of parties or brief sexual encounters). Michalos (2000) reviewed changes over the past decades in the status of women in Canada and their implications for violence against women. He found contradictory trends such that movement toward greater equality on some indicators such as school attendance was offset by concurrent movements toward less equality on other indicators, such as real average annual wages (over a period of 70 years; from 1920 to 1990, the smallest gender wage gap in which women made 60% of what men were making was in 1990, not smaller than it already had been in 1930). More important, none of the increases in gender equality seemed to protect Canadian women against sexual assault: Crime statistics suggest that instead of going down, sexual assault rates nearly tripled from 47 per 100,000 population in 1983 to 126 in 1990[1] (Michalos, 2000). Such changes may in part be due to increased reporting of sexual assault, but as most rapes remain unreported, the higher rates may reflect actual increase in sexual assault. At the very least, this finding is a reminder that improvements in women's social status do not neatly translate into less violence against them.

If all status indicators were highly intercorrelated, this would suggest that different dimensions of status such as good chances in health, nutrition, education, work, marriage, inheritance, etc., were based on a consistent cluster of social practices. Instead, the lack of correlations (even if some of it were due to measurement) suggests that the social practices underlying each status dimension form multiple, inconsistent, and contradictory patterns. Thus, the clusters of decisions and actions that result in not aborting girls, feeding girl children well, giving them good health care, sending them to school, treating them fairly in school, giving women access to jobs, paying them equal wages, granting them freedom to marry and divorce, etc., may to some extent be unrelated, or at least not perfectly correlated. An anecdotal note in the *Economist* magazine

[1] This time period (not the rates) also includes the date of the Montreal massacre (December 6, 1989), in which a male gunman shot and killed fourteen female students who were training to become engineers.

illustrates this (*Economist*, 2010). The magazine noted that in South Korea, the school system is merit based and does not discriminate against girls, many of whom do well at school. At the same time, many workplaces discriminate against women, and women face social pressures to quit their jobs when they have children. This has led to a noticeable pattern of highly qualified young women taking jobs with (relatively less sexist) foreign companies (Siegel, Pyun, & Cheon, 2010).

One example of a society with little or no wife-beating is the Wape in Sandaun Province, Papua New Guinea (Mitchell, 1999). For Wape society, Mitchell reports that, contrary to violence in many other Papua New Guinean societies, men's violence against wives was rare and that he knew of no case in which a husband had beaten and injured his wife, despite several social practices that are often thought to correlate with wife-beating (such as wives leaving their family of origin and living with their husband). Mitchell also reports that during his fieldwork, he never saw physical fights among men, women, or children. He listed several practices that set the Wape apart: a peaceful and conciliatory ethos concerned with defusing conflicts before they can escalate; little separation of the sexes, with women and men sharing public and private space and women not being secluded during menstruation; men routinely providing childcare; and boys transitioning into manhood without needing to drastically sever their ties with mothers and sisters. Mitchell also reports strong bonds of solidarity among the women in the hamlet in which he lived.

Watson-Franke (2002) discusses societies in which male rape of women is rare or unknown, including the Iroquois and Apache in North America, the Ashanti in West Africa, the Oceanian societies Nagovisi and Vanatinai, and the Mosuo in southwest China. She notes that several cultures see raping as inconsistent with high-status masculinity. One practice Watson-Franke discusses in detail concerns women's publicly acknowledged ability, and responsibility, to confer group membership and citizenship status on children. According to this analysis, in matrilineal societies "women situate the next generation socially, historically, economically, and politically," thus diminishing "the need for the certainty and authority of paternity" (Watson-Franke, 2002, p. 603). Where mothers shape the public identity of children, mothers are equally important for girls and boys, boys are not expected to sever their relationships with their mothers (Stoeltje, 1995, cited in Watson-Franke, 2002), and in the transition to manhood boys realign their relationships with their mother but are not pressured to repudiate it (Roscoe, 1991, cited in Watson-Franke, 2002). Similarly, Allen (1986) notes high respect accorded to mothers among the Keres of the southwestern pueblos where "mother" is a term of respect used to honor chiefs; and Sault (1985) notes the significance of women in the institution of godparenthood among the Zapotec.

From the material compiled by Watson-Franke (2002) and Counts et al. (1999) emerge several broad categories of gendered practices that seem to support nonviolent heterosexual relationships and that are particularly relevant here. They include practices that acknowledge women's adulthood or full citizenship (rather than treating women as wards of fathers or husbands) (Brown, 1999); practices that support women's ability to form coalitions and that underpin women's economic livelihood (Pyles, 2006); and practices that support men's ability to disrupt abusive male hierarchies and implement sanctions for perpetrators.

Brown (1999) uses the term acknowledged adulthood in reference to societies that consider women autonomous adults and that are less likely to engage in or condone violence against women than societies that regard women as less than autonomous (e.g., as "children" or as men's property). Watson-Franke (2002) sees public support for women's acknowledged adulthood reflected in practices in which men acknowledge the authority and autonomy of women. As part of these patterns, fathers have more freedom to be affectionate role models to their sons. Ideas of authority are not connected to sexuality and "heterosexual interaction does not become associated with authority, dominance, and control" (Watson-Franke, 2002, p. 605). An idea similar to acknowledged adulthood also appears in the notion of the "inviolability of the individual," which Greenfeld (1996) uses to describe child-rearing and family life among the Mountain Apache. Women, men, and children alike are seen as autonomous decision makers who have the right to make their own decisions and whose decisions ought to be respected. Considering these practices of public acknowledgement extended in equal measure to women and men, it will become clear that this is different from romanticized notions of womanhood in which abstract ideas of virtuous women are held high, whereas real women are treated poorly (Kwiatkowska, 1998).

Another set of practices concerns coalition building. Brown (1999) argued that the widespread observation that older women are less likely to be beaten than younger women is not about age per se but that older women have more extradomestic support at their disposal, from having built – over the years – coalitions with community members who can come to their rescue and having adult children (including adult sons) who can do the same. Levinson (1989) found that the presence of all-female work groups was associated with less frequent wife-beating. Such groups can function as economic resources and political alliances. Coalition building also includes active engagement in public life and the ability to shape public agendas and debates and push for changes in problematic social practices on all levels of governance, in local councils, towns, state, and national governments.

Coalition building becomes difficult when women are isolated from potential allies. Isolation could be a consequence of abuse but could also be related to other aspects of women's lives such as being homeless, in prison, or a migrant worker. However, geographic isolation per se does not seem to turn women into targets for violence. Stølen (1996; quoted in Brown, 1999) reported very little wife-beating among geographically isolated farmsteads in rural Argentina, which is possibly due to strong norms against wife-beating. Baumgartner (1993) reported that where norms favor the continuation of strong bonds between families of origin and their adult daughters, allies for women are more readily available than where community norms call for the disruption of such bonds. Thus, for women's protection, the mere existence of social ties is not sufficient; women-supportive norms and worldviews need to be lived through such ties.

Two additional sets of practices concern third-party responses to perpetrators. One concerns informal sanctions for perpetrators, which are broader than criminal justice sanction and range from gossip to open expressions of disdain for the abuser (from family, neighbors) to informal retaliation. The other perpetrator-oriented pattern concerns disrupting violent masculinities (Connell, 2005; DeKeseredy, 1990) and the often male-dominated hierarchies that control women's sexuality. In many societies, norms and conventions have evolved that link male and family standing and respectability to narrowly prescribed notions of women's virtue, modesty, and chastity. This is currently discussed mostly with regard to Islamic societies (Sen, 2005), but obsession with controlling women's sexually is evident also in Christian and other societies, although the agent(s) doing the controlling may be different (family members, doctors, mental health professionals, opinion makers, agents of the state) (Nathanson, 1991). Thus, there are connections between the control of women's sexuality – through pressure, coercion, or overt violence – and the efforts of family members to be respected within the hierarchies and worldviews that form their predominant reference points. In most societies, men have been granted more sexual autonomy than women and women's sexual autonomy has been seen as a threat to society whereas men's has not (Nathanson, 1991). These oppositional constructions of gendered autonomy tend to be entwined with worldviews that view individual autonomy as a threat to social cohesion (except for the personal autonomy of high-ranking individuals).

Rogoff (2003) suggested that hierarchical models of social relations, such as those that have traditionally dominated European and European-derived thinking, see personal autonomy as a threat to societal interdependence, whereas numerous indigenous societies see personal autonomy as its foundation. Rogoff (2003) believes that Marquesan child-rearing practices can illustrate this: "Marquesans value group participation but reject the idea of persons submitting to authority. Young children learn that autonomy is valued and then learn when and how to exercise it while still being group members" (Martini & Kirkpatrick, 1992, p. 218, quoted by Rogoff, 2003, p. 201). Thus, being a valued member of a group is not constructed in opposition to being an autonomous individual. Similarly, gender relationships can be constructed as interdependent and complementary (e.g., among the Hopi) (Schlegel, 1977). It is possible to combine personal autonomy with community orientation without developing ruthless individualism on the one hand or autonomy-crushing collectivism on the other.

This leaves open the question of how grievances are resolved in social contexts that prohibit the use of violence. In this regard, nonviolent societies offer another lesson, and this is that nonabuse is a matter of continuous, everyday, collective effort, not one-time expert intervention or a state of effortless peace. Studies of peaceful societies suggest that nonviolence is an active and continuous negotiation of structural power relations along with elaborate practices to resolve conflict and grievances (Bonta, 1997). This can include stressful and dangerous practices in which individual members of society put themselves at considerable risks (for instance, through suicide attempts as an instrument of public shaming) (Mitchell, 1999). Nonviolence is not passive bliss but hard work expressed in patterns of social practices that are fraught with ambiguity and doubt and entail ongoing efforts to deal with tension and friction, avoid escalation, and work through conflicts and disputes without recourse to violence (Bonta, 1997).

CONVERGENCE WITH RESEARCH IN THE WEST

Brown (1999) argued that a central aspect of societies without wife-beating is public acknowledgment that women confer full adulthood on girls and boys. This analysis may, at first glance, appear to be of little relevance to Western nation states but there are rather striking parallels when looking at studies of the development of public adulthood in men who become sexually violent toward women.

Lisak and Roth (1990) suggested that unincarcerated rapists' hostile attitudes toward women, and their readiness to rape women, were related to growing up in an environment that emphasized normative male authority but where, in practice, fathers were mostly absent, and the authority of mothers who were present was devalued. Similarly, Sanday (2007) linked rape proneness among young men (and their readiness to humiliate and devalue women) to their growing up in environments in which they are expected to break their bond with their mothers in order to assume full manhood. Lefkowitz (1997) offered an analysis of family dynamics that may underpin a "rape culture" (Buchwald, Fletcher, & Roth, 2005). Lefkowitz researched a case in which teenage boys who were respected high school athletes had gang-raped a neighborhood girl who was mentally retarded. The rapists had come from heterosexual, two-parent families living in a tranquil American suburb. Examining connections among male privilege, dominance, and sexual aggression, Lefkowitz concluded that the rapists had come from families in which "manly" fathers guided boys into adulthood, and females (mothers, sisters, and female teachers) were expected to be subservient to the needs of men and boys and were treated with contempt. Mothers were present but socially and culturally devalued; "respectable" masculinity was associated with devaluing women (Lefkowitz, 1997).

Drawing on different empirical evidence, Hanmer (2000) offered a similar analysis. Her study included interviews with sixty women of different social and cultural backgrounds in England who had suffered the sort of domestic violence Johnson (2008) termed intimate terrorism. According to Hanmer, the perpetrators of this abuse gained advantages from being abusive that were interrelated with the statuses they enjoyed as males, sons, husbands or partners, and fathers. By being abusive and getting away with it, the perpetrators were "both a primary force in the construction of social life characterized by degradation, humiliation and personal harm, and the upholder of deeply held cultural values which make it very difficult to effectively intervene in [their] violence" (Hanmer, 2000, p. 11). Hanmer (2000) further argued that the

> maintenance of family hierarchy and male privilege within the family group conflicts with interventions to control violence against women and children. Prioritizing men, their needs, wants and desires means tolerating behaviors that would not be permitted from lower-status members of the family groups, namely, women and children. The primary modes for handling the conflict that arises between the valuing of non-violent behaviour towards wives and children and the valuing of men in hierarchically organized family group relations are to not

> know of or, if knowledge is inevitable, to view the matter as private... The point of these strategies adopted by others outside the marital pair is to avoid making a value judgement on his behaviour and to avoid the need to intervene, thus leaving intact values supporting gendered family hierarchies. (p. 20)

These practices of "not knowing" and denial were also observed by Lefkowitz in the responses of the rapists' elders, who rallied around the boys and denied their crime.

Hagemann-White et al. (2010) undertook a detailed and comprehensive review of empirical evidence on the perpetration of different forms of violence against women. According to this analysis, individuals develop into perpetrators through multifactorial pathways that defy simple explanations. Much of the research focused on factors measured at the individual level (such as attitudes, personal biography, or stress). However, none of these factors are sufficient causes for perpetration. "For the vast majority of individuals, these factors will only lead to violent behaviour when there is a conducive context permitting or encouraging this outcome" (Hagemann-White et al., 2010, p. 78). Whereas we assign moral and legal responsibility for perpetration to individuals, societies create the context that is conducive to abuse or able to resist it.

The evidence just discussed suggests that rape and domestic violence against women are absent or rare where societies uphold – in spirit and in practice – women's right and ability to decide how they wish to conduct their domestic and sexual relationships with men. This is not only a matter of having laws on the book or noble ideologies, but to a good extent the upholding of such rights and ability occurs through the everyday actions of third parties in families, communities, and workplaces.

The notion that these third parties would expect and welcome women to decide how to regulate their sexual and domestic relationships with men is contrary to the historical gender traditions in most societies, the West included. For third parties who believe that families or societies require hierarchical rule of men over women, the idea of autonomous women is unnerving because such autonomy is read as undermining male advantage or destroying the fabric that holds society together. Yet, although this view has been widespread, it is neither inevitable nor universal. On the contrary, in some societies, autonomous women are integral to societal welfare, and personal autonomy is thought to be the beginning of social cohesion, not its end.

NAMING ALTERNATIVES TO ABUSE

Where does this leave the issue of naming nonabuse in the positive? Does it really matter if we talk about nonviolence without naming positive alternatives? To some extent it does because as expressions of recognized social practices the nonwords (nonviolence, nondiscrimination) fall short; they do not specify what to do, only what not to do. Knowing what not to do does not automatically imply knowing what to do instead. Alternatives to abuse in gender relations are not automatic defaults that kick in once abuse ends. Rather, they are gendered practices that need to be created in an active process of culture making, and this includes conceptualization and naming. In the absence of such deliberate effort, words and metaphors will be imported from other fields of practice including, ironically, the practice of warfare ("combating domestic violence").

Lakoff and Johnson (2003) argued that our conceptual system "is fundamentally metaphorical in nature" (p. 3) so that metaphors structure our language, thinking, and action. If this is so, then the use of violent metaphors in antiviolence work is problematic (eradicating, stamping out violence) because these metaphors might interfere with the flourishing of nonabusive thought and action. The intent behind using expressions like "combating violence against women" may be to emphasize the urgency of the issue, but such usage has its problems. It would be a shame if urgency and determination could be conveyed only by recourse to military language. More important, if metaphors structure thought and action, then violent metaphors would keep thinking about nonviolence locked in frameworks of violent practices, which might limit the envisioning, conceptualization, and implementation of alternative practices.

Anthropologists and linguists have discussed words and phrases in different languages that express worldviews for which there may be no compelling expression in English (popularized in dictionaries of "extraordinary" words from around the world) (Jacot de Boinod, 2006; Moore, 2004; Rheingold, 2000). The lack of a positive English word for nonviolence may reflect, as Kurlansky (2008) suggested, a lack of collective recognition of nonviolent social practices. Where violence is used to dominate and enforce, nonviolence implies a willingness to tolerate, give-and-take, respect, and resolve issues without force. Several indigenous North American languages appear to have expressions that reflect such values, some of which English-speaking anthropologists have rendered as "inviolability of the individual," in which individual includes women, men, and children (Greenfeld, 1996, pp. 491–2), *Pi um i'*, a Hopi expression roughly meaning "it's up to you" (Titiev, 1944, cited in Greenfeld, 1996) or *t'áá bee bóholníih*, a Navajo expressions meaning "it's up to him to decide" (Lamphere, 1977, cited in Greenfeld, 1996). The French term *laissez-faire*, also used in English, perhaps comes close. However, within traditions of hierarchy and subordination, the term *laissez-faire* also has connotations of neglect and mayhem (which it might not have in egalitarian traditions).

Lepowsky (1993) applied the term "egalitarian ethic" (p. 38) to societies in which every adult can participate in prestigious activities (not everyone may be good at it, but everyone has the opportunity to do it). Among the Vanatinai, women have central positions in kinship webs, own land and valuables, control the distribution of the fruit of their labors, and control access to wealth, prestige, and influence. Again, however, egalitarian ethic should not be confused with passive bliss. Rather, Lepowsky found that the result of this ethic is "continuous competition for status and influence . . . precisely because Vanatinai society is egalitarian and without ascribed positions of status" (p. 39).

Women around the world have struggled to publicly name rapes and beatings as violence and to speak against euphemisms such as domestic disturbance. The public acknowledgement of forced sex and beatings as abusive and violent has been an important step toward social change (Donat & D'Emilio, 1992; Kelly, 1988). Feminist naming of abuse was grounded in an analysis of gender relations in which individual acts of cruelty against women (and children) were seen as an expression of the abuse of societal power vested in men and the lack of societal power vested in women. Without such an analysis, the word violence loses much of its significance. When violent actions are no longer seen in the context of social power relations, all violent acts become alike: Differences between attack and self-defense disappear as do differences between the fear some women feel when attacked by their male partner and the ridicule some men express when attacked by their female partner. The feminist movements have formulated public critiques of exploitative gender relations based on patriarchal gender orders (Hagemann-White, 2003). In these critiques, sexual and domestic violence were made visible and publicly denounced as expressions of gender relations characterized by male control over women in family and intimate relationships, male entitlement to women's sexual and domestic services, and an ethos of valuing particular forms of maleness (heterosexual, above all, and domineering) combined with devaluing women and femaleness (Connell, 2005).

This analysis effectively revealed abusive gender relations, but has done less for rethinking nonabusive heterosexual gender relations. In the absence of alternative language, metaphors are borrowed from other fields of practice: In the term healthy relationships, the (desirable) notion of health is imported from medicine and public health. The use of respect in the term respectful relationships is intriguing as established practices of respecting seem largely associated with different forms of hierarchy in which respect is due to those at the top but not necessarily to those at the bottom. Healthy and respectful relationships do name nonabusive relating in the positive, but perhaps it would be good if they were temporary placeholders until terms emerge that are grounded in actual egalitarian gender practices that invoke not only desirable outcomes but also the continuous effort that led there.

To throw a third choice into the mix, this book refers to nonabusive gender relations as *considerate.* This choice is the result of consulting the dictionary; not exactly evidence of socially grounded practice, but it yielded a positive word. The *Random House College Dictionary* (1975) defines considerate as "1. having regard for another's feelings, circumstances, etc. 2. carefully considered, deliberate." The two meanings echo (faintly) the notion of valuing the other and of effort involved in nonviolent relating.

Nonetheless, picking words from the dictionary is an unsatisfying solution. What is needed is a critical analysis that links considerate gender relations to nonpatriarchal gender orders, similar to the feminist analyses that have linked abusive gender relations to patriarchal inequality and injustice. It is inconceivable how raping, coercing, hitting, and humiliating could be seen as occurring within otherwise unproblematic gender relations. Instead, such abuses constitute exploitative, perverse forms of relating. In their place need to be qualitatively different practices of gender relations in which ruthlessness, cruelty, domination, and control have no place. Articulating and naming these qualitatively different gender relations need to occur in reference to actual positive gender practices. Peaceful societies have managed to maintain nonviolence not merely as the professed norm but as realized, daily practice, and they offer alternative vistas on the relationship between gender ideologies and gender practices. They also offer insight into principles of gender relations and third-party practices that can inform shifts in these practices in societies in which sexual and domestic violence is common. The following chapters examine how informal third parties – family members, friends, co-workers, and neighbors – participate in social practices that create contexts conducive to abuse and how they contribute to contexts resistant to abuse.

3

The Informal Construction of Women's Sexual and Domestic Autonomy: Networks, Beliefs, and Personhood

Informal responses are part of the local contexts in which sexual and domestic violence occur, in which abuses may be thwarted, and in which their aftermath unfolds. Through action and inaction, informal third parties position themselves in relation to societal practices that delineate what is possible for women and men in heterosexual relationships. Hanmer (2000) argued that the "most basic factor constituting the cultural framework that either fully or partially legitimates home-based violence by men against women is that the boundaries specifying correct behaviour for women are not those that bind men to society and cultures, however diverse these cultures may be in other ways" (p. 11). Informal responses contribute to the drawing of these boundaries, but in doing so they have some leverage. As shown in the previous chapter, societies can draw boundaries of acceptable behavior that benefit both women and men and grant all individuals the right and freedom to enjoy autonomy, respect, and considerate, interdependent relationships.

As the following chapters show in more detail, informal third parties have the ability to marshal material and symbolic resources that can benefit victims or perpetrators and that have implications for recovery, accountability, and future abuse. To support victims, informal third parties can provide shelter, money, transportation, or childcare as well as moral support and consolation or a safe place to sort out what happened and think about the future. Third parties can also mobilize resources on behalf of the perpetrator by protecting him from criticism and interference or helping him to thwart attempts at investigation and prosecution. The social support literature, by and large, has emphasized positive responses from social network members, but to what extent social support actually is forthcoming may depend on the nature of the issue for which it is needed (Taylor, 2007). For instance, the research examined in Chapter 5 shows that network responses to sexual and domestic violence are ambivalent, including help, criticism, and denial. This ambivalence also is evident with regard to disagreements in intimate dating relationships in which same-sex friends are seen as the most reliable allies and parents are seen as a source of both support and criticism (Klein & Milardo, 2000).

The ability of informal third parties to influence the trajectory of sexual and domestic violence is grounded in several aspects of human relationships. One aspect concerns the structure of social ties within which informal responses exist, which is discussed by drawing on network research and the ecological framework. The second aspect concerns informal third parties as important reference groups who have clout in shaping and transmitting the social construction of gendered responsibility for sexual and domestic violence. This is examined in relation to beliefs in rape myths and domestic violence myths. The third aspect concerns the significance of other people in influencing our sense of self. With regard to this aspect, insights from psychoanalytical work are used to illustrate that the emergence and maintenance of a healthy self has relational dimensions, which means that recovery from trauma also depends, at least in part, on the quality of relationships with other people. These three aspects are interrelated and together they shape the informal social context in which victims and perpetrators go about their daily lives.

INFORMAL RESPONSES WITHIN THE STRUCTURE OF SOCIAL TIES

Sexual and domestic violence against women are "located in particular sets of social relationships, structures of power, and meanings of gender" (Merry, 2009, p. 3). Informal responses do not occur in a social vacuum but within webs of relationships and in relation to the conduits of power and influence that these relationships constitute. Informal third parties participate in these conduits of power to different effects. The goal of this analysis is to contribute to a more detailed "situated analysis [of gender violence] that recognizes the effects of the larger social context on gender performances" (Merry, 2009, p. 3). Such an analysis acknowledges that "the formal structures of male dominance do not fully indicate the intricate network of power relationships within any particular culture, and [that] attention has increasingly focused on more informal relationships of power influence and prestige" (Frymer-Kensky, 1992, p. 120). More specifically, the accounts of women who suffered domestic violence "provide information on how hierarchy and privilege is structured within [their] families, how cultural boundaries apply to men and women, how individual women negotiate within and move beyond culturally and socially prescribed limits on their behaviour, and how individual men maintain their socially superior position without altering their behaviour" (Hanmer, 2000).

Intimate, heterosexual relationships are embedded in networks of social ties with family members, friends, neighbors, co-workers, and others (Milardo & Wellman, 1992). These networks have structural features, which may be significant for the provision of support (including their size and the closeness among network members) (Milardo, 1988). Informal networks may also be linked to formal power when network members hold powerful positions in the community, the state, or the workplace, or when friendships or other social ties connect them with influential people.

Only a few studies have examined the structure of social networks of women in abusive relationships. In the United States, Hoff (1990) interviewed nine women who had experienced domestic violence along with 131 members of their social networks in order to examine how "social network members (family, friends, neighbors, health and human service workers, clergy, police) [function as] the practical avenues for expressing and reinforcing a society's values and beliefs about women, marriage, the family, and violence" (p. 11). In terms of the relationship between network structure and network support, Hoff hypothesized that optimal network support would be forthcoming when networks were dense and close knit (network members know each other or are on friendly terms); when the networks included a number of different types of relationships (family, friends, neighbors); if network members would be responsive when asked for help and able to reach the victim quickly if needed; and network responses would be helpful (emotional support, information, material aid). Against this ideal, Hoff examined the actual, reported network characteristics and impacts. Although no woman reported such an ideal network, Hoff found numerous instances of informal support from male and female network members (see Chapter 5).

Michalski (2004) argued that "domestic violence endured in large part because the social structure of interpersonal relationships within societies continues to provide the fertile conditions that spawn and perpetuate the use of violence" (p. 653). He points to anthropological evidence suggesting that women who have strong support from family and kin are less vulnerable to domestic violence. For example, Baumgartner (1993) explored whether young brides who leave their family of origin and move in with their husband's kin become more vulnerable to abuse from husband or in-laws than if they stayed with their families of origin. Under such arrangements, young women would be on their own in a strange family and cut off from the protection of parents, older siblings, or other family members. Brown (1999) argued that patrilocal marriage customs make young women vulnerable to abuse from their husband's mother for whom a young daughter-in-law may be one of the few persons in the household over whom she has any power. However, in his cross-cultural analysis, Levinson (1989) did not find an association between residence pattern and wife-beating (see Chapter 2). Then again, perpetrators often deliberately manufacture their victim's social isolation by preventing her from seeing family or friends and by discouraging others to visit. Thus, isolation can be a deliberate control strategy (Pence & Paymar, 1993). As further evidence of a network structure that seems conducive to abuse, Casey and Beadnell (2010) found that male youth with dense, mostly male peer networks reported higher rates of abuse against a female partner than male youth with less dense networks of male and female friends.

Yet, structure alone does not sufficiently explain how informal third parties respond. Baumgartner (1993) concluded that it is not the configuration of social ties per se that predicts whether family members come to the defense of their daughter, sister, or niece but the nature of the norms and values that go along with these ties. If a woman's family subscribes to the belief that once she leaves to live with her husband she has severed all ties to her origin, they are unlikely to come to her aid. Yet, if they continue to think of her as belonging with them and deserving their protection and support, they are more likely to come to her aid. Watson-Franke (2002) also emphasized the interplay of social ties and value systems in her analysis of why in some societies men do not rape women, arguing that these societies avoid the consolidation of patriarchal power in one man who is simultaneously husband and father with rights over wife and daughter. Rather than focusing on network structure alone, it seems more likely that both social ties (structure) and social norms (content) matter. More specifically, this seems to be a matter of how network members interpret existing norms and how they position themselves in relation to victim, perpetrator, and other third parties who uphold those norms.

Bronfenbrenner (1979) viewed the webs of social ties surrounding people as a social ecology, a notion he used to analyze the social and interpersonal context of child development. He thought of this ecology as composed of interlinked social spheres that directly and indirectly influence the child. For instance, Bronfenbrenner posited a so-called microsystem in which child and parent interact and parents influence children directly. In addition, parents also interact, in the mesosystem, with others such as teachers. Through what teachers tell parents about their children, teachers may indirectly influence children through the parental interpretation of what the teacher said. Thus, the mesosystem influences the microsystem, which is possible because there is a linking pin that is part of both systems (in this case the parent). Microsystem and mesosystem are not separate worlds but interrelated spheres of social influence.

Over time, the ecological framework became a tool for organizing findings drawn together from different disciplines. When it became clear that rape and domestic violence defy single-cause explanations, the ecological framework helped to represent "violence as a multifaceted phenomenon grounded in an interplay among personal, situational, and sociocultural factors" (Heise, 1996, pp. 263–4). Yet, what is particularly intriguing about the original notion of the ecology of the developing child is the interplay *between* spheres of social influence. This interplay is also relevant for intimate abuse against women

The social ecology of victims includes microsystems such as the relationship with the perpetrator or with a friend as well as mesosystems such as relationships between perpetrator and his peers, or between friends and others who might be able to educate friends about the dynamics of abuse. Activity in these mesosystems can have implications for the microsystem: If peers encouraged the perpetrator or failed to confront him, they could make matters worse for the victim (DeKeseredy, 1990; see Chapter 6). If a victim's friends understand that coping with domestic violence can take a long time (which they might have learned through interactions in the mesosystem of their relationships with teachers or by listening to a victim support specialist), they may be able to support the victim through a longer period of time (see Chapter 5). If a woman who lived with an abusive husband was isolated from supportive friends, lived instead with his kin who blame her for the abuse, and worked in a place where her employer threatened to fire her because she cannot concentrate at work, her social ecology would include multiple mesosystems that would make coping with the abuse particularly difficult.

Thus, what from the outside appear to be separate social worlds (friends, family members, workplace) in fact constitute a multifaceted "niche" (Bronfenbrenner's term for an individual's unique social environment) made up of interconnected patterns of third-party responses. Practices in the mesosystem (such as endorsement of rape myths or acceptance of violence against women), through their influence on practices in the microsystem (treatment of women in intimate heterosexual relationships), shape, limit, or open opportunities for women's safety and redress.

Furthermore, networks of kin and friends coexist with formal power structures in local communities, in the workplace, and on the level of national governance, resulting in complex and potentially contradictory webs of power, in which third-party responses create different opportunity structures (Lepowsky, 1993). A woman may be able to engage the legal system on her behalf, even while her local community refuses to support her. On the other hand, local "old-boys" networks, in which perpetrators are friends with the very police officers who could wield state power over them, can cut women off from a crucial source of formal support from police (Websdale, 1998). Thus, mesosystems may constitute critical links between gendered practices of relating in the microsystem of victim and perpetrator and gendered practices in the macrosystem of institutions (at work, in school, in the community).

The notion of social ecology is useful to draw attention to these links and their potential implications. What is less useful about the notion of ecology (originally used in biology) is the connotation that social ecologies are environments in which impersonal natural forces are at work, rather than deliberate social policy. A concept more prominent in debates about social policy and political influence is the notion of community (Kelly, 1996). Sentimental views of community conjure images of neighbors watching out for each other. These can mask tensions between the rights of women and men in a community that is grappling with sexual and domestic violence in its midst. These tensions may be aggravated when relationships between communities are difficult and multiple systems of oppression intersect (Crenshaw, 1991; Incite! Women of Color Against Violence, 2006; Mama, 2000; Sokoloff & Pratt, 2005; Thiara, Condon, & Schröttle, 2011).

Kelly (1996) argued that communities are not given but are constructed based on place, interest, work, identity, or shared political experience, which means that debates on the role of community in sexual and domestic violence need "a framework that begins from an analysis of power relations, rather than an ideal type [of community] that stresses consensus, shared history and values. Relationships of dominance and subordination are present in families and kinship networks, in localities and institutions, making the achievement of community much more complex than previously envisaged" (p. 72).

As an example of a community response that has successfully addressed both sexism and racism, Kelly (1996) cites Southall Black Sisters (SBS), a black women's group in London who argue that "although racism is a primary concern for black people, their communities are not unified and women and men's interests are not necessarily the same. SBS has highlighted the silencing of women's voices and experiences in areas where religious leaders are accepted as speaking for the community. SBS has [challenged] racist policing and, at the same time, insisted that the police respond to domestic violence as a crime in their community" (Kelly, 1996, pp. 75–6).

Informal responses occur within these complicated community contexts, and informal third parties may find themselves in a situation in which, in order to support a friend or family member who is a victim of abuse, they would need to challenge prevailing norms in the family or the community. Thus, informal third parties may incur backlash and criticism from other network members (in the mesosystem, in Bronfenbrenner's terms). Yet, when third parties, perhaps in an attempt to enact community cohesion, conform to local sexist norms they instead are likely to contribute to an even deeper isolation of the victim, and thus effectively fragmenting the community by marginalizing the victim (see Chapter 5). Reflecting on experiences in Australia, Holder (1998) wrote that in many communities "family is considered as the critical unit upon which communities grow. Finding ways of acknowledging this <u>and still</u> condemning violence is also challenging indigenous and non-indigenous people in this country. And further – acknowledging this and still maintaining both a critical focus on the family and asserting women's rights to define themselves outside of it may be a challenge for feminists in the future" (pp. 7–8; emphasis in the original).

Moreover, how third parties respond to a victim also has implications for the perpetrator. When victims are blamed for rape, perpetrators are likely to receive less, if any, punishment (Temkin & Krahé, 2008). In contrast, where the victim is supported by influential allies, the perpetrator may find it more difficult to avoid accountability. However, these contingencies are not clear-cut matters. Victims may be supported, and perpetrators still not held accountable, or both victim and perpetrator may be punished. Informal responses are not "surgical" interventions; they are woven into, and actively weave, a complex fabric of interpersonal relationships and social ties, in which they contribute to the "messy and contradictory nature of gender ideologies and gender-related behaviors" (Lepowsky, 1993, p. 34). Any one response may have only a minor impact and responses may work at cross-purposes – support from a friend may counter blame from a parent, and revenge from the perpetrator can undermine help from victim allies.

GENDER BELIEFS: INFORMAL ASSIGNMENTS OF RESPONSIBILITY AND BLAME FOR GENDERED ABUSE

The construction of responsibility and blame for gendered abuse are reflected in rape myths (Bohner et al., 2009; Burt, 1980), domestic violence myths (Peters, 2008), and so-called honor-based justifications for violence against women (Sen, 2005). These constructions have in common that they define sexuality and family life in ways that severely restrict women's autonomy, that excuse (or consider necessary) sexual and domestic violence against women by husbands, boyfriends, or family members, and that blame women for abuse suffered at the hands of others.

Believing in rape myths means assuming that rape does little harm, that the victim probably is largely or fully responsible for having been raped, and that the perpetrator carries little if any responsibility (Bohner et al., 2009). The effects of belief in rape myths have been well documented (Horvath & Brown, 2009). For example, studies with prospective lawyers and jurors have shown that belief in rape myths influences decision making about rape cases. When presented with scenarios of rape cases that include factual evidence about the details of the case, lawyers and jurors who believe in rape myths tend to ignore this factual evidence and instead base their assessment of the case on preconceived notions of victims and perpetrator; in other words, even in the light of contrary factual evidence they blame the victim (Temkin & Krahé, 2008; Krahé et al., 2008). Belief in rape myths is widespread and thought to operate similarly to schematic knowledge structures in that rape myths tend to override factual evidence of rape (Gerger et al., 2007).

In psychological research, beliefs in rape myths are measured as individual-level variables but they have social roots and social effects: We hear them from others, and we might repeat them to others. By articulating and spreading rape myths and victim-blaming beliefs, third parties contribute to the construction of gendered and racialized assumptions about who is to blame in sexual and domestic violence and who deserves leniency or punishment (White, Strube, & Fisher, 1998). Belief in rape myths delineates the moral universe in which people's full personhood and rights are respected and honored (Opotow, 1990): Through rape myths, victims are excluded from this moral universe, whereas perpetrators remain within. Thus, sharing heterosexual rape myths and domestic violence myths is not merely about problematic content held in individual minds but constitutes a social practice of denying full personhood to women (Horvath & Brown, 2009; Romito et al., 1997). When third parties believe in such myths, their actions are likely to influence victims and perpetrators in different ways, from critical remarks, to overt blame, protection for perpetrators, and dismissal of victims' attempts to seek redress.

Rape myths have been identified in media representations, literature, pornography, religious teachings, and the law (Allen et al., 2006; Edwards et al., 2011). How the presence of rape myths in such discourses influences individual decision making is another question. From the perspective of social cognition research, rape myths may activate ("prime") victim-blame and minimization of the harm done through rape. There is some evidence that when they have been primed, rape myths correlate more highly with rape proclivity (respondents indicating they would have raped a woman as described in a vignette of a rape) than when they have not been primed (Bohner et al., 2005). Thus, victim-blaming and rape-dismissive bits of dialogue, imagery, or text embedded in TV shows, pornography, or Bible stories may activate rape myths in the heads of viewers and readers.

A third-party perspective brings an interpersonal dimension to this discussion. Similar to other knowledge structures, rape myths may be formed and spread through interaction (Morgan, 1986). In addition, to the extent that these interactions take place within personally significant reference groups (friends, peers, respected family members), rape myths may not only be primed (become more accessible cognitively) but may also be fused with perceived or real social pressure to trivialize rape, exonerate perpetrators, and blame victims (Berkowitz, 2003).

Morgan (1986) viewed dyadic relationships as links between shared knowledge structures and social networks. He focused on knowledge structures in general but his arguments seem relevant for victim-blaming beliefs as well. Morgan suggested that "participation in personal relationships [contributes to] the production of 'shared knowledge structures', i.e. partners in a relationship not only possessing the same information, but also organizing and interpreting it in a similar fashion" and that "the creation of shared knowledge structures depends upon the information available within social networks" (p. 404). This approach illustrates how victim-blaming beliefs may be shaped, energized, and spread in the mesosystem of relationships among friends, acquaintances, and other third parties in the social networks of victims and perpetrators.

This interpersonal grounding may be one reason why rape myths are highly resistant to individual-level interventions such as jury instruction and educational programs (Bohner et al. 2009). If rape myths are thought of as collective practices organized in socially shared knowledge structures, then interventions that fail to address their interpersonal dimension might be less successful than interventions that do. If rape myths persist (at least in part) because they are grounded in social relationships, interventions would need to address the interpersonal and relational dimension of victim-blaming beliefs. In a psychological study on legal decision making, Krahé, Temkin, and Bieneck (2007) found that lawyers who thought they would have to explain their judgments about a rape case to a jury based their judgments less on rape myths and more on case facts than lawyers who did not expect to have to justify their response. Thus, the mere expectation that one's decision would be judged by others undermined the impact of rape myths on decision making. According to the social-cognition literature, such public accountability motivates people to pay more attention to actual evidence and thereby reduces the kind of schematic information processing in which decisions are based on preconceived ideas rather than on factual evidence (Lerner & Tetlock, 1999).

Regardless of whether spreading rape myths or domestic violence myths is motivated by active hostility to women, by a desire to fit in, by a matter of mindless repeating what friends and family members are saying, the practice is not harmless but has negative effects on victims (see also Chapter 5).

PERSONHOOD: RELATIONAL DIMENSIONS OF SELF AND COPING WITH TRAUMA

Research has focused primarily on the positive and negative effects of informal responses on victims. Positive responses such as reassuring victims or providing practical support tend to have beneficial impacts and support safety and recovery, whereas unsupportive responses that shame and isolate victims can cause further harm (Ullman, 2010) (see Chapter 5). In addition, informal action or inaction toward the victim has implications for the perpetrator or other third parties. When third parties shun a victim who has been raped, they not only harm the victim but they also send a message to the perpetrator (and others) that the problem lies more with the victim than with the perpetrator. If peers or kin side with the perpetrator, they contribute to isolation of the victim.

An example of such dual effects emerged from interviews with women in the UK who were reflecting back on the process of resettling after leaving abusive relationships (Abrahams, 2010). A critical moment in the transition to life without the perpetrator turned out to be the first night alone in a new home, which for some women was so intensely anxiety producing that they felt vulnerable to attempts by perpetrators to lure them back. An evening visit by a friend or neighbor might defuse anxiety sufficiently to shore up women's resolve to manage on their own, while derailing the perpetrator's attempts to regain control over the woman.

Psychoanalytical work suggests that informal responses influence a person's sense of being worthy and capable; a healthy sense of self is built on a foundation of good relationships with others (Winnicott, 1965). Winnicott, a British pediatrician and psychoanalyst, was concerned with the relationship between child development and what he called the "facilitating" environment. He thought that the caregiver's activity of "mirroring" (loving responsiveness to a child's being) is central to the development of children's healthy sense of self and others and contributes to the foundations of an individual's autonomy and ability to interpret and participate in the world. American psychiatrist Herman (1992) applied this perspective in work with victims of intimate abuse and argued that recovery from trauma is also a social and relational achievement. This psychoanalytical work is referenced here because it suggests how deep the impact of informal responses can go. Both approaches help to show how profound the impact of informal responses can be as they reach to the very foundations of personhood. When third parties respond to disclosure of abuse with awkward silence, ridicule, or blame, they may strike at the core of the victim's being.

Informal responses affect the outlook of victim and perpetrator by impacting their respective sense of self as valued members of society. Such spirit and positive outlook are similar to the concept of self-esteem, but the latter is often treated as something that can be shaped by individual effort alone, which might be misleading. The research considered here argues that the foundation of self-esteem is social esteem – an interactive achievement to which third parties have much to contribute.

Herman (1992) was concerned with the relational bases of trauma and recovery, in particular trauma suffered from sexual or domestic abuse. She argued that recovery from the trauma is not just an individual but also an interpersonal accomplishment.

Although it is the survivor who attempts to recover, the process of recovery can be assisted by other people, and Herman might argue that it has to be assisted by other people in order to be complete. Third parties can contribute to recovery, if they assist the survivor in resolving what Herman called the *dialectic of trauma* – the dilemma of struggling to forget the abuse and struggling to tell it:

> The conflict between the will to deny horrible events and the will to proclaim them aloud is the central dialectic of psychological trauma. People who have survived atrocities often tell their stories in a highly emotional, contradictory, and fragmented manner which undermines their credibility and thereby serves the twin imperatives of truth-telling and secrecy. When the truth is finally recognized, survivors can begin their recovery. But far too often secrecy prevails, and the story or their traumatic event surfaces not as a verbal narrative but as a symptom. The psychological distress symptoms of traumatized people simultaneously call attention to the existence of an unspeakable secret and deflect attention from it. This is most apparent in the way traumatized people alternate between feeling numb and reliving the event. The knowledge of horrible events periodically intrudes into public awareness but is rarely retained for long. Denial, repression, and dissociation operate on a social as well as an individual level. The study of psychological trauma has an "underground history." Like traumatized people, we have been cut off from the knowledge of our past. Like traumatized people, we need to understand the past in order to reclaim the present and the future. Therefore, an understanding of psychological trauma begins with rediscovering history. (pp. 1–2)

For Herman, recovery from trauma is about "restoring connections: between the public and private worlds, between the individual and community, between men and women" (pp. 2–3).

Thus, she emphasizes the concurrent personal, social and cultural dimension of responses to trauma and to what medicalized discourses often view as "individual" problems (Humphreys & Thiara, 2003).

Psychoanalytical approaches have been criticized for ignoring power relations and promoting victim blame; integrating psychoanalytical and social–structural analyses can be challenging (Haaken, 2010). The position taken here is that informal responses in relationships and social networks forge a link between individual psychodynamics, social relationships, and structural power relations and that the psychodynamic consequences of social interactions are particularly significant in the context of structural inequality. The "second injury" (Symonds, 1980/2010) that is inflicted on rape victims when their claims are dismissed or belittled has consequences for the balance of power in the microsystem of victim and perpetrator and in the mesosystem of relationships between perpetrator and third parties. By blaming the victim, third parties redistribute significant symbolic assets: Denying the victim a positive outlook and prestige concurrently pays a dividend to the perpetrator because his responsibility is partly or wholly lifted and his outlook shored up. Reassuring a rapist that he need not worry about being held responsible because she was drunk, a slut, or otherwise insignificant, exploits society's sexist prejudices, in a single stroke, to his advantage and her disadvantage. From this perspective, seemingly private responses of informal third parties play into, reinforce, or challenge relations of power connected to structural inequalities.

Through relationships and social networks, friends, family members, and others assign and lift blame, give and deny help, strengthen and weaken self-worth and social standing, and thus engage in social practices that contribute to the informal construction of women's sexual and domestic autonomy.

DATA, EVIDENCE, AND INTERPRETATION

In this and the preceding chapter, several lines of research were used to create a conceptual framework for analyzing the impact of informal responses on sexual and domestic violence against women. The basic argument is that informal third parties contribute to the social construction of women's autonomy (or lack thereof) in their sexual and domestic relationships with men and that this is largely a matter of everyday practices. In the next three chapters, more empirical data on informal responses are examined and used to shore up this basic argument. However, although these data document various aspects of informal responses, they were not necessarily collected to show how informal third parties construct women's autonomy. Can they then still be interpreted in terms of women's autonomy? It is argued here that they can because data are not the same as evidence of something; They become evidence only in light of an interpretive framework. Without interpretive guidance data, "do not tell us what they are evidence for" (Lloyd, 2005, p. 242). That is, without an interpretative framework, the meaning of data remains unclear. That also means that the meaning of data may change when the interpretive framework changes. For instance, what does it mean when empirical data show that women who left an abusive partner returned to him? When the interpretive framework posits that leaving is better than staying and will end abuse, then these data could be taken as evidence that the abuse is not that bad or that she does not know what she wants. When the interpretive framework posits that leaving can be risky and may not end abuse, then the same data could be taken as evidence that the time for a complete separation has not yet come or that leaving could create more problems than staying.

The empirical data examined in Chapters 4, 5, and 6 can be sorted into different groups. One group includes studies on what informal third parties said or did about the abuse, including documentation of responses to victims, to perpetrators, or to both. Most of this evidence comes from interviews with female victims of male intimate violence. This includes studies in which women described to whom they mentioned the abuse or whom they approached for help and what informal third parties said or did in response. In many studies women were contacted through domestic violence agencies (Goodkind et al., 2003; Moe, 2007; Rose, Campbell, & Kub, 2000), in some they were contacted through adverts in the community (Levendosky et al., 2004). Another group includes studies in which victims were asked to describe their social networks. A third group is victimization surveys in which respondents were asked to identify people or agencies to whom they disclosed abuse without further information about how informal third parties responded (Kilpatrick et al., 1992) (see also Chapter 1). A fourth group of studies produced empirical data on the presence of other victims or perpetrators in the social networks of victims and perpetrators. This includes studies in which perpetrators were asked to describe their social networks (DeKeseredy, 1990; Raghavan et al., 2009). Very few studies have interviewed informal third parties directly (Hoff, 1990; Latta & Goodman, 2011).

What are these data evidence for? Depending on the authors' theoretical perspectives, these data have been interpreted as evidence of help-seeking, social cohesion, social support, disclosure dynamics, bystander intervention, coordinated community response, intervention strategies, network structure, and mental health impacts. These are valid ways to interpret these data, but they are not the only ways. The data can also be interpreted within a framework concerned with women's sexual and domestic autonomy. Thus, empirical data on helping, listening, blaming, and so forth can also be read as evidence of the informal construction of women's sexual and domestic autonomy. Or, more specifically, as evidence of the interplay of social ties, gender beliefs, and the construction of personhood – a triad of societal forces that, considering the lessons from egalitarian societies, is significant for understanding how societies grant (or fail to grant) women the right and ability to decide how to conduct their sexual and domestic relationships with men.

4

Disrupting Assaults

This chapter examines informal responses when third parties are present during an abusive episode. Domestic violence and rape are often thought to happen "behind closed doors," hidden from public view. A majority of these crimes indeed are not reported to the authorities, but that does not mean that nobody else knows about them. On the contrary, in many cases, family members, friends, co-workers, or neighbors are in the area where the assault occurs and can see or hear it (Planty, 2002). To assume that sexual assault and domestic violence typically occur without witnesses is misleading; instead, it is important to acknowledge the third parties who may be present as well as their efforts to intervene and to explore how formal interventions might interface with informal attempts at disrupting assaults so that these are successful and both witnesses and victims remain safe.

This chapter first examines findings from crime victimization surveys, which show that third parties indeed are often present during intimate assaults. However, such surveys offer little detail about the circumstances of these episodes and the ways in which third parties try to disrupt them. More informative in this regard are two other lines of inquiry. One of these concerns children's interventions in episodes of domestic violence against their mothers;

the other concerns college student interventions in the buildup to sexual assault at college parties. These lines of research have developed in relative separation from each other and employ different conceptual frameworks and methodologies. Yet both shed light on this aspect of informal responses and both illuminate important policy implications and complications.

PRESENCE OF INFORMAL THIRD PARTIES DURING INTIMATE ASSAULTS AGAINST WOMEN

Crime victimization surveys have estimated how common it is that third parties are present during different types of crimes. This is often done with an interest in whether the presence of witnesses increases the reporting of crime to authorities. As just mentioned, many scholars have concluded that intimate violence against women is hidden from public view (Felson, Messner, & Hoskin, 1999), but this claim is valid primarily with regard to the fact that these crimes are hidden from the view of the police; they are much less hidden from the view of family, peers, or co-workers.

Using data from the U.S. National Crime Victimization Survey (NCVS), Planty (2002) estimated that in 29% of sexual assault incidents and in 36% of intimate partner violence incidents, an informal third party was present (third parties were even more often present in nonintimate violent crimes). This suggests that, although about two-thirds of intimate assaults may occur without witnesses, in a sizable one-third of incidents witnesses may be present. For sexual assaults in the United States from 1993 to 1999, this would mean that in over 100,000 cases the assault was witnessed by a third party (Planty, 2002) – intimate assaults are not, by nature, crimes without witnesses. (It should be mentioned that in the NCVS, third party was understood to include "eyewitnesses, bystanders, instigators, interlopers, other household members, and police officers" [Planty, 2002] so that, strictly speaking, a formal third party could have been included among informal third parties.)

According to the NCVS data, the presence of a third party only minimally increased reporting to police. In 44% of all incidents of violent crime in which a third party was present, the crime was reported to police, compared with 41% with no third party present. Perhaps a meaningful difference, but one that is dwarfed by the underreporting of violent crime in general: More than half of the violent incidents were not reported to police at all. Felson and Paré (2005) examined informal reporting of intimate partner violence to police using data from the U.S. National Violence Against Women Survey. They concluded that third parties were "unlikely" to report assaults by an intimate partner to police and that in particular sexual assaults by acquaintances are likely to go unreported. Yet these third parties knew of the assault. Using the same data set, Chen and Ullman (2010) found that 17.7% of physical assaults were reported to police by the victim and 7.4% by a third party (three-quarters of these incidents were not reported to police!). Sexual assaults were reported even less frequently (although reforms to rape statutes may have encouraged reporting when comparing reporting levels before 1974 and after 1990 [Clay-Warner & Burt, 2005]).

The U.S. NCVS also asked victims to assess the impact of third-party action when third parties did intervene. From the victim's point of view, in 35% of intimate partner victimizations third parties improved the situation, in 44% of incidents intervention had no effect, and in 12% of incidents it made things worse (because the perpetrator became even more violent). Improvement was due largely to preventing injury to the victim either by helping the victim escape or by scaring off the offender (Planty, 2002). Thus, in a substantial number of incidents informal intervention in an abusive episode helped the victim.

A different perspective on witnesses comes from studies that ask third parties directly, typically neighbors or community members, and this research is often framed in reference to community relations or social cohesion. Paquin (1994) surveyed 650 households in Kentucky on whether there had been spouse abuse among the neighbors. About 10% of participants said that they had "strongly suspected" domestic violence next door, and about 5% had provided "respite." Frye (2007) used data from a community sample of 119 people in New York City to examine whether neighbors are more likely to intervene in instances of violence when they think of their neighborhood as a cohesive community. Frye found no relationship between perceived social cohesion and reported likelihood of informal intervention. In Spain, Garcia and Herrero (2007) used data from a nationally representative sample of nearly 15,000 adult Spaniards to examine the relationship between reporting domestic violence against women to police and perceived social disorder in the neighborhood. They concluded that third parties are averse to reporting when they perceive disorder as high. From these studies, the relationship between crime reporting and community cohesion is inconclusive; it may vary with differences in measurement and the wider sociocultural context.

However, what is clear from the preceding findings is that general crime surveys (at least for the United States) corroborate findings from shelter studies that informal third parties often are aware of abuse and in many cases actually are present during abusive episodes. The findings also suggest that informal witnesses are not necessarily passive bystanders but try to come to the victim's aid. When they do so, they often make things better for the victim. Unfortunately, in some cases, interference backfires because perpetrators step up their violence, with some risk to third parties as well as to victims.

The U.S. NCVS set the lower age limit for persons to be counted as third party at 12 years. In many instances of domestic violence, witnesses are younger than that, as the next section explores.

CHILDREN'S INTERVENTIONS IN DOMESTIC VIOLENCE

The debate about children who witness domestic violence against their mothers has been framed largely in terms of children's exposure to domestic violence and the traumatic stress suffered from such exposure, along with health impacts and mitigating factors that support resilience and recovery (Holt, Buckley, & Whelan, 2008; Hunt, Martens, & Belcher, 2011; Vickerman & Margolin, 2007). However, even as children are worried and stressed (and at risk of being assaulted), they also engage in numerous strategies to protect themselves, comfort their mothers, distract the perpetrator, and call for help (Edleson et al., 2003).

Children see or hear domestic violence because they are either in the same room as the adults or next door. Children have reported seeing domestic violence even when their parents claim that the children did not see it (O'Brien et al., 1994). U.S. police reports of domestic violence investigations revealed that where children had been present during the incident, more than one-fourth of children called for help (girls slightly more often than boys; the average age of these children was 8 years [Fusco and Fantuzzo, 2009]). In a U.S. study of mothers and children who were in emergency shelters after fleeing highly violent homes, most children had tried to intervene on behalf of their mothers (Jarvis, Gordon, & Novaco, 2005). In a Swedish study, children aged 12 to 15 years talked about what they used to do when their fathers assaulted their mothers and described how they would try to distance themselves from the violence (e.g., turning on music, trying to read), comfort or protect their mother, distract or appease their father, or call others for help (Överlien and Hydén, 2009). Överlien and Hydén (2009) concluded "that children need to be taken seriously as social agents and as active constructors of their own social worlds" (p. 480). Studies in England also documented that children try to disrupt domestic violence by physically intervening between father and mother (Mullender et al., 2002). Sometimes very young children offer support: McGee (2000) described a 5-year-old boy comforting his mother after his father had assaulted her.

Considerable detail on how children intervene in domestic violence comes from a study by Edleson et al. (2003). The researchers asked mothers who were experiencing domestic violence from their male partners how their children intervened in violent episodes. All women in the sample were approached through domestic violence projects in which they and their children were receiving services. Interviews were anonymous, by telephone, and focused only on incidents that occurred within the 12 months prior to the interview. A total of 114 interviews were collected. The average age of the women was 34 years at time of the interview; about half of the women were white, one-third were African American, about 10% were Latina, and another 10% were Native American and other ethnic and multiethnic groups.

The women reported a range of interventions by their children. Over half of the women said that, at least occasionally during an episode of violence, the children yelled from the same or another room, and 21% of the women said that the children called someone else for help. About one-fourth of the women said their children, at least occasionally, physically intervened in a violent episode. The study also found patterns in children's interventions: Children intervened relatively more often when their mothers were unemployed, had less education, were not married to their abuser, and lived in transitional housing. Children intervened more when the abuser was not their biological father and when they lived with their mother. Children also intervened more the older the abuser was. Children intervened more physically the higher the level of abuse and impact of abuse on their mothers. The study shows that children's interventions are not unusual and that they use a variety of different strategies depending on interpersonal, social, and economic circumstances. In another U.S. study, Allen et al. (2003) found that children who witnessed abuse against their mothers showed similar emotional responses but differed in their actions, which ranged from doing nothing or trying to avoid or ignore the abuse to becoming aggressive against the perpetrator, seeking help and protecting mothers.

For mothers who experience domestic violence, a decisive factor to seek help, including help from formal authorities and service providers, is the fact that their children are exposed and suffer as well (Meyer, 2010). The policy response should facilitate mothers in this step, not make it more difficult by threatening legal action for failure to protect children against the perpetrator (Weithorn, 2001). One of the major protective factors for children exposed to domestic violence against their mothers is having a close relationship to a supportive adult; in most cases this is the mother (Holt et al., 2008). To give children the help and protection they need, they need to be helped and protected together with their mothers, not at the expense of their mothers.

Even when service providers believe that it would be best to help both mothers and children, they may struggle to articulate how exactly this could be done (Letourneau et al., 2011). Domestic violence services, child protective services, and regulations for child contact and visitation have developed on different trajectories and created contradictory legal worlds (Eriksson & Hester, 2001; Hester, 2009). Despite efforts to bridge these worlds (see Kracke

& Cohen, 2009, for the U.S. systems) and calls for a more systematic integration of institutional practices (Hamby et al., 2010) the policy response, in many countries, remains fragmented, and intervention at the expense of abused mothers is unlikely to benefit their children (Douglas & Walsh, 2010; Goodmark, 2010; Hester, 2010; Humphreys, 2010).

STUDENTS' INTERVENTIONS IN SEXUAL ASSAULTS AT COLLEGE PARTIES

A different perspective on informal disruption of abusive episodes comes from research with college students. Whereas the studies on children's interventions in abuse against their mothers document what children actually do, the campus studies – a more recent field of research – are more about what students might do if properly trained. Most studies are evaluations of programs in which college students are taught how to recognize and disrupt the buildup to a sexual assault against another student (Potter & Banyard, 2011). This research, for the time being, appears to be mostly North American in origin (Anderson & Whiston, 2005; Schwartz & DeKeseredy, 1997; Söchting, Fairbrother, & Koch, 2004).

The incidence of sexual violence against female students is relatively high in the United States and Canada (Fisher, Cullen, & Turner, 2000; Schwartz & DeKeseredy, 1997) but this is not much different from the UK (National Union of Students, 2010) or Australia (Sloane & Fitzpatrick, 2011), and U.S. rates may even be lower than those elsewhere (Fisher & Wilkes, 2003). As of yet, there is little comparable, international research, but this is changing.[1]

[1] http://fra.europa.eu/fraWebsite/research/projects/proj_eu_survey_vaw_en.htm.

What is different in the United States is a research and legal context that for decades has put sexual assault on campus on the agenda of policy makers and forced campus officials to implement policies and programs aimed at reducing or preventing sexual violence (Armstrong, Hamilton, & Sweeney, 2006).

The first representative U.S. study found that 2% of female students had experienced unwanted intercourse and that 44% of female students reported unwanted sexual contact (Koss, Gidycz, & Wisniewski, 1987). The incident of rape during 1 year (number of rapes, rather than number of women raped) was 353 rapes (involving 207 women, meaning some women were raped multiple times during 1 year) out of a sample of 3,187 women (or about 111 rapes per 1,000 female students). About a decade and a half later, Fisher et al. (2000) put the estimate at 35.3 rapes per 1,000 female students in a given academic year. In Canada, DeKeseredy and Kelly (1993) estimated that about 45% of female students had had unwanted sexual experiences (including rape and attempted rape) since leaving high school.

For one university in England, Fisher and Wilkes (2003) estimated that 6% of students had experienced rape or sexual assault over a period of 9 months (this included male and female students). A national UK survey by the National Union of Students estimated that 14% of female students had experienced a physical or sexual assault while they were a student at university (a longer time frame than in the Fisher study) and nearly 70% had experienced some form of sexual harassment (National Union of Students, 2010). A survey in Australia found that 12% of female students had experienced attempted rape, 17% completed rape, 67% an unwanted sexual experience, and 9% had been hit or physically mistreated (Sloane & Fitzpatrick, 2011).

In the United States, rape-prevention programs at college campuses have a long history framed by research and legislation dedicated specifically to the issue of sexual assault on college campuses, and over the years a variety of intervention strategies have been used (Karjane, Fisher, & Cullen, 2005; Koss & Oros, 1982; Koss et al., 1987; Sloan, Fisher, & Cullen, 1997). One recent approach is so-called bystander programs that teach students to intervene in the buildup to a sexual assault.

Bystander programs address students as potential bystanders rather than as potential victims or perpetrators and thus are an example of educational programs deliberately designed with informal third parties in mind (Banyard, Plante, & Moynihan, 2004). In the terminology of routine activities theory, bystander programs aim to turn peers into "guardians" (Schwartz et al., 2001), a term with complex connotations. It was perhaps chosen to capture the idea that students can look out for each other but it is also reminiscent of the term chaperone, which in turn is associated with the control of unmarried women's sexual activity. This is not to dismiss the importance of "guardians" but to highlight the challenges that arise when trying to safeguard another person's sexual well-being, without controlling or restricting her (or possibly his, depending on context) personal autonomy. Bystander programs rest on three assumptions: There will be more bystanders than rapists at a party; rapists engage in preparatory activities that lead up to the actual rape and can be detected; and numerous factors keep bystanders from intervening, which can be addressed through proper training.

The first assumption is based on research suggesting that the majority of men on campus do not rape (or at least they say so) and that most sexual assaults on campus may be perpetrated by a relatively small number of repeat rapists (Lisak & Miller, 2002). Lisak and Miller (2002) found that among 1,882 male students, 44 (2.3%) admitted to a single act qualifying as completed or attempted rape and 76 men (4%) admitted to multiple acts qualifying as completed or attempted rape. This suggests that most male students (about 94%) do not rape (which says nothing about other unwanted sexual activity) and that the vast majority of admitted rapes (439 of 483 or 91%) were committed by repeat offenders.

The second assumption concerns the presence of peers "during the pre-assault phase where markers of sexual assault risk are present" (Burn, 2009, p. 1). Markers of sexual assault risk include a woman going to a private location with a male acquaintance, friends leaving a woman alone at a party, intoxication of potential victim, perpetrator, or both, and men displaying "pre-rape behaviors" (e.g., touching women against their wishes, making inappropriate sexual jokes, hostility, acceptance of violence) (Rozée and Koss, 2001). Such markers could be warning signs of impending abuse, and recognition of warning signs is an important element in early intervention.

The third assumption is based on research about bystander intervention in emergencies, which posits that situational barriers keep third parties from intervening (Latané & Darley, 1970). Central in this research has been the notion of an "unresponsive bystander" who is kept from helping by barriers such as not being sure the event is an emergency and not knowing how to intervene (Latané & Darley, 1970).

The unresponsive bystander has been imagined as somebody who has the option to ignore the emergency and walk away from it and who is unconstrained by social ties to either victim or perpetrator (unlike children witnessing their mother being abused). Latané and Darley (1970) proposed this model following the brutal rape and murder of Kitty Genovese in New York City in 1964 during which presumably unresponsive neighbors watched and did nothing. However, this appears to have been a misinterpretation of the actual circumstances of the Genovese murder. According to later research, nobody watched the entire incident and several neighbors in fact intervened, which included calling police and ambulance

(Manning, Levine, & Collins, 2007). However, the killer was determined (he wanted to kill a woman, according to his own testimony) and made sure outside interference would be extremely unlikely (by acting late at night and mostly out of sight). Help arrived, but too late; Kitty Genovese died in the ambulance.

Most of the early research on bystander intervention ignored sexual and domestic violence and focused instead on helping in a variety of nonemergencies (such as mailing a lost letter) and on intervention in emergencies such as accidents or fire breaking out (Latané & Darley, 1970; Stürmer & Snyder, 2010). For these situations, the bystander model postulates that decisions to intervene follow a sequence of steps: People need to notice the event, conclude that intervention is needed, take responsibility for intervening, decide how to intervene, and then do it. At each step, intervention can be derailed. Subsequently, this model has been applied to bystander intervention in abuse, including reporting child abuse (Hoefnagels & Zwikker, 2001) and sexual assault at college parties (Banyard, 2008).

Bystander training can raise awareness and impart intervention skills, but most evidence of the effectiveness of such programs has relied on participants' self-reports (rather than observations of actual bystander behavior) and, as with other rape-prevention programs, it is unclear whether bystander training reduces victimization or perpetration rates (Söchting et al., 2004).

Burn (2009) found that when students self-reported high barriers to intervention they also said they would be unlikely to intervene, lending some support to the notion of barriers to helping. Female students were asked about intervening to protect a victim; male students were asked about intervening to stop a potential perpetrator. Burn also found that men, more than women, said they would be less likely to help if the victim was "unworthy" (measured by victim-blaming statements such as being less likely to help when the victim would have made choices that increased risk, was intoxicated or provocatively dressed), a finding that echoes other studies on helping behavior in which bystanders were more likely to help when they thought the victim deserved it (Stürmer & Snyder, 2010; West & Wandrei, 2002).

Brown (2010) surveyed about 400 male college students about the relationship between attitudes supporting sexual aggression and willingness to intervene and found that what predicted willingness to intervene were not men's own attitudes but what they thought other men were thinking. This lends some support to the idea of "social norming," an approach developed for college student populations that is based on the premise that students engage in problematic behavior in part because they perceive peer pressure to do so and assume that their peers also engage in these behaviors. Especially when the behavior in question is not public, such assumptions may be wrong; social-norming campaigns try to correct them and thereby reduce perceived peer pressure. This approach is common in programs to reduce alcohol and drug abuse and has been applied to sexual assault prevention (Berkowitz, 2003).

McMahon (2010) surveyed over 2,000 first-year students and found that those who scored higher on rape-myth acceptance reported lower willingness to intervene. Among other findings, men, students entering a fraternity or sorority, athletes, and students without prior education about sexual assault displayed more beliefs in rape myths. Reported willingness to intervene was greater among women, students who had had prior education about rape and students who knew somebody who had been raped. The findings, while preliminary and based on correlations among self-reports, do suggest barriers to intervention, but these barriers seem less situational as envisioned by Latané and Darley (1970) and more structural in that they are related to respondents' social locations and awareness of social issues.

A special issue of the journal *Violence Against Women* recently presented several bystander program evaluations in the United States. Katz, Heisterkamp, and Fleming (2011) assessed the Mentors in Violence Prevention program (bystander approach within a gender justice framework) with high school students. Compared with high school students in a control group, those who participated in the program reported that they found a wider range of behaviors wrong (e.g., a student making sexual advances on someone who is drunk) and that they would intervene if the need arose. In a study of sorority members, the women who participated in the Bringing in the Bystander program reported higher confidence and intent to intervene if necessary than sorority members who did not participate in the program (Moynihan et al., 2011). Male students who participated in a program that combines bystander and social-norming approaches showed desired changes in some self-reported measures (such as finding sexually aggressive behavior less rewarding) but not in others (such as acceptance of rape myths) (Gidycz, Orchowski, & Berkowitz, 2011). Male participants in yet another program did report less rape-myth acceptance as well as more willingness (and efficacy) to help than nonparticipants (Langhinrichsen-Rohling et al., 2011). A theater-based program increased participants' beliefs that bystander interventions are effective and that participants would intervene compared with nonparticipants (Ahrens, Rich, & Ullman, 2011). Finally, participants in the Green Dot program reported less rape-myth acceptance and more bystander behaviors than nonparticipants (Coker et al., 2011). Neither of the studies assessed actual bystander behaviors; all relied on self-reports, which by and large showed promising results but are inconclusive about behavioral differences between program participants and others.

While the bystander model is experiencing a surge of interest among those working on campus sexual assault, assessment of the model in other contexts is lackluster. Although the barriers to helping postulated in the model are well documented in empirical research on intervention in nonviolent incidents, it appears to lack practical relevance as researchers have been "unable to use it to increase the likelihood of helping in emergencies" (Levine & Cassidy, 2010, p. 222). Research on college bystanders may still prove this conclusion wrong; the college party context may be a setting in which the situational barriers (or barriers with similar effects) that Latané and Darley had in mind exist and where they can be addressed by teaching students to recognize and overcome them. It is less clear whether the model lends itself to other contexts of intimate violence against women.

Incidentally, it is curious that the Genovese case became a foil for theorizing bystander intervention rather than a case of, say, marital rape or sexual harassment in the workplace or spontaneous helping from peers (such as the case quoted at the beginning of Chapter 1), which might have made social and personal relationships among victim, perpetrator and third parties more central. It is also odd that in the social psychological literature the gendered, and indeed misogynist, nature of the Genovese case, in which a man deliberately set out to kill a woman, received little attention. Instead, the case was interpreted in terms of unrelated actors (perpetrator is a stranger; bystanders are strangers; urban alienation) and abstract questions about human nature (are people basically selfish or altruistic?). In this way, the Genovese case was used to conceptualize emergencies as ungendered disasters that happen to strangers, which had the effect of excluding from consideration as emergencies most cases of sexual and domestic violence.

In addition, helping and intervention were conceptualized as a matter of strangers having to overcome ungendered barriers, rather than friends, family members, and other nonstrangers having to act within complex social ties and attachments. And rather than speculating about ungendered human nature, the literature on help-seeking after sexual and domestic abuse suggests that gender, race, poverty, and culture shape intervention in intimate emergencies.

5

Responses to Disclosure and Help-Seeking

In terms of informal third-party actions, responses to disclosure and help-seeking have received more research attention than disruption of assaults (previous chapter) and collusion with perpetrators (next chapter). Disclosure, help-seeking, and informal responses form interrelated and at times contradictory patterns. Studies on disclosure have emphasized the immediate reactions when victims tell somebody that they have been abused, whereas studies on help-seeking have emphasized the provision (or denial) of practical help. Disclosure is often the first step in help-seeking, but not all victims who tell also seek further help; some simply want to share their story and may not need or want further support, or not yet. Some survivors may want emotional support but not being told what to do. Responses to disclosure and help-seeking can be contradictory: Women have reported being blamed and helped by the same network member or receiving blame from one informal third party and help from another (Hoff, 1990).

The chapter first addresses the patterns of abuse (adult sexual assault, patterns of domestic violence) that are disclosed or for which help is sought, as well as impacts of informal responses. Then empirical evidence of informal responses is examined along a hypothetical time line, beginning with responses to disclosure, moving on to initial responses to help-seeking during or after a crisis, and ending with longer-term issues (see also Wilcox, 2006). This is done to emphasize that disclosure and help-seeking can be lengthy processes; it does not mean that each individual case follows the same time line. For disclosure of sexual assault Ullman (2010) concluded that it is "not a one-time, all-or-none event. The nature and extent of disclosure can vary over time, and one may tell different people at different times after the assault, all of which may affect recovery . . . [and disclosures] range from minor references to fully verbalized accounts" (p. 44). For domestic violence, disclosure also may be a long process, and help-seeking can continue for months and years, as it may take women a long time to extricate themselves (and their children) from abusive relationships and rebuild their lives (Abrahams, 2010). Finally, this chapter addresses some of the challenging social contexts in which disclosure, help-seeking, and response may occur; when these contexts are blighted by misogyny, racism, or poverty, strained social networks may be hard pressed to provide comfort and aid. This chapter concludes with views from informal third parties.

PATTERNS OF ABUSE

Almost all of the research reviewed here relies on reports from victims; studies in which third parties have been interviewed directly are relatively rare (see Hoff, 1990; Latta & Goodman, 2011). Most studies of women's disclosure of sexual assault concern assault when women were adults and help-seeking after sexual assault experienced as an adult (Kaukinen & DeMaris, 2009; Ullman, 2010). This discussion does not include adult disclosure of child sexual abuse (see Everill & Waller, 1995; Sarkan, 2010).

With regard to domestic violence, many studies include women who were contacted at or through domestic violence shelters and refuges. This suggests that they had fled highly violent situations and were dealing with severe abuse that posed imminent danger to themselves or their children – the sort of abuse that has been at the center of antidomestic violence work for decades (Dobash & Dobash, 1979; Stark, 2007), and which Johnson (2008) referred to as intimate terrorism. In these cases, disclosure, help-seeking, and informal responses occur in a context in which a severely abusive perpetrator may go to great lengths to maintain control over the victim by preventing disclosure and help-seeking and deterring third parties who may try to help. This may involve threatening or manipulating potential helpers in a family or a social network, badmouthing the victim, or putting up a charming front to bring third parties to his side (Hanmer, 2000) (see next chapter).

Another set of studies examined responses to help-seeking by women who experience domestic violence but live in the community (rather than in a shelter) (Levendosky et al., 2004), and research was also done on help-seeking by women who appear to be dealing with "situational couple violence" rather than with intimate terrorism (Leone, Johnson, & Cohan, 2007). Leone et al. (2007) found that women who experienced intimate terrorism were much more likely to seek formal help from police or medical services, whereas women who experienced situational couple violence relied on help from friends and neighbors. This illustrates that help-seeking strategies are likely to be tailored to the most pressing needs of the victim. For victims of intimate terrorists, primary concerns are often about safety and safe escape, whereas victims of situational couple violence may be more concerned about ending the violence within the context of the relationship. And they may be successful in this; the processes through which abusive men desist are not well understood, but in some relationships they are responsive to their female partners and cease to abuse (Wuest & Merritt-Gray, 2008).

IMPACTS OF INFORMAL RESPONSES

One of the first in the United States to write about the interpersonal dimensions of disclosure of sexual assault trauma was Martin Symonds, a former police officer who later trained as a psychoanalyst. Symonds (1980/2010) emphasized the role of countertransference in disclosure dynamics: how disclosure and response to disclosure affect patient, therapist, and the relationship between them. Symonds noted that "ordinary professional attitudes" that were characterized by a distant and passive demeanor increased victims' shame and self-hate, making trauma worse and constituting what he termed a "second injury." Responses to disclosure may be mindless or mean spirited or devoid of warmth and empathy. Such negative responses are significant because in addition to potentially causing a second injury, they may silence the victim (Ahrens, 2006), and victims may internalize negative responses (Taylor, Wood, & Lichtman, 1983) and come to regret disclosure (Jacques-Tiura et al., 2010; Ullman, 1996). Research also has found that negative third-party responses to the disclosure of sexual violence aggravate posttraumatic stress (Ullman et al., 2007).

Disclosure of sexual assault or domestic violence is risky. What for outsiders may appear to be an obvious step toward ending abuse for victims and survivors can be fraught with difficulty and negative repercussions. Stereotyping, ridicule, and blame often undermine support for victims and create barriers that make coping and recovery more difficult. In regard to the risk of serious negative backlash, disclosure of abuse may be different from disclosure of other problems. Ullman (2010) suggested that in much of the U.S. trauma literature, it has been assumed that disclosure of trauma in general is beneficial. Indeed, at least for some survivors, this may be a motivation to disclose. For instance, Ahrens et al. (2007) quoted one woman as saying "I needed to tell her. Let it out." However, the risks of disclosure can undermine potential benefits (Symonds, 1980/2010; Jacques-Tiura et al., 2010). Fear of retribution from the perpetrator or other third parties may also discourage disclosure. Thus, disclosure is more complex than the seemingly simple act of telling might suggest. To minimize the risk of negative reactions from third parties survivors who disclose abuse may "edit" their experience, for instance, by making the abuse sound less severe than it had been (Dunham & Senn, 2000).

Positive responses, on the other hand, have significant benefits. Disclosure is more likely when survivors assume that others will be helpful (Feldman-Summers & Norris, 1984; Ullman, 2010). As discussed in Chapter 3, Herman (1992) argued that collective effort is necessary to heal trauma from intimate abuse, restore trust, and mend ruptured social relationships. In her perspective, positive informal responses are essential for recovery from trauma because personal well-being and integrity are grounded in social interactions that affirm and express recognition of the victim's humanity. This perspective is similar to the psychoanalytical concept of mirroring proposed by Winnicott (1965): Through their responses, third parties recognize (or fail to do so) the needs and accomplishments of the person who is disclosing sexual violence. Intimate abuse itself denies this recognition and, if anything, holds up a distorted mirror (to stay with the metaphor) in which the victim appears worthless. Thus, repair of the damage done by abuse involves collective affirmation of the survivor's dignity and humanity; the people called on to provide this collective affirmation are informal and formal third parties.

Not surprisingly, responding to disclosure or help-seeking can be challenging for third parties. In the professional field, vicarious trauma and secondary traumatic stress are considered occupational hazards for trauma counselors and staff in sexual assault and domestic violence agencies (Baird & Jenkins, 2003;

Johnson & Hunter, 1997). For informal third parties, too, listening to disclosures of sexual or domestic violence may be stressful, but third parties deal with this in different ways and some experience informal responding as positive and rewarding. For example, Banyard et al. (2010) found that in comparison with male confidantes, women reported more distress but also more positive responses and less confusion. Ahrens and Campbell (2000) asked friends about their experiences helping a rape survivor and found that most of them experienced this as positive.

RESPONSES TO DISCLOSURE

Rape survivors disclose for different reasons. According to Ahrens et al. (2007), these can be sorted into two broad groups. One includes disclosures initiated by survivors who are looking for support or a place to articulate their experience. The other includes disclosures prompted by a third party who senses that something is wrong or who was at the scene when the rape occurred. The search for specific support also seems to motivate many women who join online self-help groups for domestic violence survivors (Westbrook, 2007). However, in other cases, survivors disclose because circumstances were encouraging or needed explanation. For instance, Ahrens et al. (2007) reported that one woman disclosed during a conversation other people had about rape; another woman disclosed because she felt she needed to explain damage to her household that was caused when fighting back the rapist.

During the 1990s and 2000s, the number of studies, in particular in the United States, that examined rape disclosure increased significantly (see Ullman, 2010, for a detailed overview). These studies usually have found that rape survivors who disclosed encounter a mix of positive and negative reactions from informal and formal third parties. Participants in a study by Filipas and Ullman (2001) reported that, although they received both positive and negative responses from both formal and informal third parties, negative responses were more common from formal third parties whom they found to be victim-blaming, stigmatizing, and controlling and who voiced rape myths and violated confidentiality.

One study is described in more detail to illustrate the breadth and complexity of third-party responses to rape disclosure (Ahrens et al., 2007). The data come from interviews with about 100 adult women in the Chicago area who self-identified as rape survivors and who participated in a study on the impact of community services on the well-being of rape survivors (Campbell et al., 1999). About half of the participants were African American, a little over a third were white, and the others were Latina, multiracial, and Asian American.

Ahrens et al. (2007) found that positive responses were more common (61.3%) than negative responses (38.7%). However, the latter were not rare, accounting for over one-third of all responses. Positive responses included being supportive (mentioned by 29% or respondents and illustrated by this quotation: "She put her arms around me and gave me a hug"); sharing the victim's distress (19.4%); providing practical support such as taking the victim to the hospital and keeping her company through the night (5.4%); and mobilizing further support (5.4%). An example of the latter was a grandmother who found her granddaughter bloody and unconscious on the lawn and then asked an uncle to call the police.

Also coded as supportive were responses in which third parties tried to seek revenge (reported by 2.2% of respondents). Not all victims want third parties to seek revenge, but in this study the two women who mentioned revenge found it a supportive response. One of the women had a brother who beat up the acquaintance who had raped her. The other woman had a partner who threatened violence against the stranger who had raped her.

Negative responses included blaming the victim for the rape (reported by 10.8% of respondents); being unsupportive, stunned, silent, or confused (12.9%); doubting the victim's story, which included doubting that the (known) perpetrator would do such a thing (7.5%); responding coldly and detachedly (5.4%); and actively refusing help – a rare but hurtful response (2.2%) (Ahrens et al., 2007).

For one-third of the participants the self-reported impact of these responses was detrimental. Slightly less than half of the participants (46.8%) felt the responses they received had a healing impact, and 20.2% of survivors said the responses had no discernible impact. Healing impacts included feeling better (7.4%), comforted (11.7%), supported (9.6%), validated (6.4%), and being able to unburden oneself (9.6%). A third of the women felt worse after disclosure: They were hurt by the third-party responses (25.5%), or angry (5.3%), or felt responsible for making the third party feel bad by talking about the rape (4.3%) (Ahrens et al., 2007).

As might be expected, receiving negative responses was associated with more detrimental impacts, whereas receiving positive responses was associated with no detrimental impacts. More surprising were differences between the responses of informal (friend, family, partner, co-worker, neighbor, or stranger) and formal third parties (police, doctor, therapist, or clergy), depending on who had initiated the disclosure. Responses from informal third parties were always more positive than negative, regardless of who initiated the disclosure. In contrast, responses from formal third parties were more positive when a third party had prompted the disclosure but more negative when the survivor had initiated it. More specifically, these were cases in which the women had disclosed a rape to police or a doctor and in which they received proper case processing and medical procedures yet felt left alone with the burden of their traumatic experience.

Yet, when formal third parties had initiated the disclosure, their subsequent responses were experienced as supportive and helpful. In one case, a therapist probed for more detail from the client's past, which encouraged the woman to disclose a rape, even though it had not been the reason for the therapy, and in response the therapist was very supportive. In another case, police had been called to the scene and had validated the survivor's story.

Instances of ambivalent and less than helpful professional responses were reported in other studies as well (Filipas & Ullman, 2001; Golding et al., 1989; Ullman, 1996). However, it is unclear why formal third parties were experienced as helpful when they encouraged disclosure but not when the survivor asked for help. Perhaps those who prompted disclosure were more prepared to "mirror" the survivor's humanity and were aware that such support and validation are needed in addition to following professional protocol.

Judgmental attitudes and victim-blaming also occur when domestic violence is disclosed. In an Italian study, Romito and colleagues (1997) found that family members were not particularly helpful to women experiencing domestic violence. Out of eighteen women, only two reported support from family; in one case from a father, in the other case from a sister. For six women, parents who might have helped lived too far away or were no longer alive. In the case of nine women, family members, when asked, refused to help; these family members de facto took the side of the perpetrator (Romito et al., 1997).

In a comparison of women's experiences in Britain and the United States, Kirkwood (1993) found that only a minority of informal third parties were able to listen to the victim with an open mind and supportive attitude. Where that was the case, women appreciated such support because it helped them to sort through their experience, develop their own understanding of it (rather than having to submit to somebody else's interpretation), and regain a sense of self. Yet many other women felt that only limited understanding was forthcoming from their network members. This was either because they refused to believe that the woman had been abused, thus denying the woman's reality, or because they pressured her to adopt views that made no sense to her in light of her experience of domestic violence (such as saying that all couples get into arguments at some point).

In particular, three negative dynamics stood out. In one, network members judged women based on stereotypical views of domestic violence (such as assuming that physical beatings were to be expected or dismissing the seriousness of emotional abuse). In another, network members got tired of hearing about the abuse and its aftermath but rather than saying so (and owning up to their own struggle with the issue) they implied that the woman should feel differently. In the third dynamic, network members avoided the topic of abuse; women would say something minor about relationships to test if the other might support her need to talk but received a blank stare in return or the other person would change the topic. The net effect of these three dynamics was silencing: The women stopped talking about the issue.

In addition to these negative responses, for some women disclosure was complicated in other ways. One woman felt extremely embarrassed about the abuse, which made her reluctant to disclose, which in turn made it more difficult for her to sort through her experience. One lesbian and one black woman felt that speaking out about abuse would be read by other lesbians and blacks as criticism or even betrayal of the lesbian and black communities, respectively. Struggles against prejudice and oppression from white, heterosexual majorities had put a heavy emphasis on solidarity among minority communities, which left little room to address abuses that occurred within them (Kirkwood, 1993).

INITIAL RESPONSES TO HELP-SEEKING

As with responses to disclosure, responses to help-seeking tend to be mixed: Some are very supportive, others are not. Help-seeking, too, is a complex process in which victims have to consider the potential benefits and risks of engaging their networks (and formal resources). Victims "read" their environment before deciding whether and whom to ask for help (Kirkwood, 1993). Help-seeking is made more difficult when third parties ignore hints and warning signs or when they signal that they are not able or willing to help. It is made easier when third parties are sensitive to cues and signal that they are ready to help if needed.

Some forms of help may be easy, such as passing on the phone number of a domestic violence project or rape crisis center. In other cases, helping may be more difficult. The needs of women in shelters, in particular, may be significant, including childcare, housing, financial aid, transportation, and protection against a perpetrator who may be very violent (Goodkind et al., 2003; Moe, 2007). In addition, perpetrators may pose danger to potential helpers. But help-seeking may be difficult for other reasons, too. The very abuse for which help may be necessary may be nearly invisible to both victims and third parties. Brutal, physically violent acts may be recognized more easily as abusive, but more subtle forms of coercive control may be so normalized that they are not recognized as abusive. For instance, possessive jealousy may be interpreted as a sign of love rather than of control (Römkens & Mastenbroek, 1998; Wood, 2001).

Although many women are resourceful in coping with domestic and sexual violence and, in particular when abuse is severe, seek out the support from domestic violence projects or police (Bowker, 1983; Gondolf, Fisher, & McFerron, 1990), help-seeking success depends on how third parties respond when approached for help. To some extent this may be a matter of structural features of social networks (Michalski, 2004), such as the number of potential helpers in the network, where helpers live, and how far away they are. It is also a matter of beliefs and attitudes: As Baumgartner (1993) argued, the mere existence of network members is no guarantee that victims will find support because potential helpers may refuse support or side with perpetrators (see Chapter 3).

Informal third parties are often in a position in which they may offer immediate support or act as gatekeepers to other resources or formal services. In the late 1970s in Britain, Cavanagh (1978; cited by Kelly, 1996) proposed that women who were experiencing domestic violence seek help from informal networks first and approach formal support systems only when informal networks are not able to deter the offender or provide sufficient support to the victim. Findings from two relatively early studies, both concerned with domestic violence, are described in more detail to illustrate the breadth and complexity of informal helping.

In the United States, Hoff (1990) undertook a detailed analysis of the social networks of nine women who had dealt with domestic violence. Help from family and friends included "emotional support, guidance, shelter and protection, money, rides, car use, baby care, and more" (p. 90). Hoff found several cases of considerable support. In one, two brothers traveled 1,500 miles to help their sister escape from her abuser. Other help was perhaps meant well, but the victim felt it was counterproductive (one friend encouraged her to drink alcohol to cope with being upset). In other cases, informal third parties confronted the perpetrator on behalf of the victim. One mother-in-law confronted her own son about his abuse of his wife; and one woman's neighbor took her perpetrator to court (Hoff, 1990).

In other cases, the responses from informal third parties were a mixture of support, criticism, and rejection. One woman told Hoff that her mother and sister had rescued her from an abusive relationship but that her father did not want her in his house. Once the immediate crisis was over, the sister blamed her for having married the abuser in the first place (Hoff, 1990, p. 91). Another woman contrasted support from a loyal friend with victim-blaming comments from family members and was disappointed that nobody in her family confronted the abuser. One woman reported that she stayed at her aunt's house and asked the aunt's husband to protect her against an abuser who had threatened to kill her. The aunt's husband reportedly simply walked away from the woman, which for this woman was the most disappointing informal response because it left her feeling completely alone although over twenty network members lived in her immediate neighborhood (Hoff, 1990).

Kirkwood (1993) interviewed nineteen U.S. and eleven British women about the process of leaving abusive relationships. Interviews took place at least one year after the abusive relationships and focused on, among other topics, the reactions from friends and family and the usefulness of their responses. Housing, financial support, medical advice and service, physical safety, and emotional safety were important needs. Because in most cases leaving the relationship meant leaving the residence the women shared with the abuser, finding alternate housing was a major challenge and one-third of the women stayed with friends or family for a period of a few months to a year. One of the women reported that for her this informal support was a literal life saver that prevented her from committing suicide. However, for other women, staying with friends and family added yet another layer of distress as it meant living in crowded conditions, having to adapt to different lifestyles, while lacking the freedom and support to deal with their intense emotions (Kirkwood, 1993).

Network members helped in different ways. Some were supportive listeners, and many played an important role in the women's safety plans. For example, they foiled the abusers' attempts to track down the victim by keeping her true location secret, either pretending they did not know where she was or by giving the abuser false leads. In one case, friends and neighbors made changes to the woman's house so that it looked as though she lived in it. Her abuser launched attacks against the house, while she was safe elsewhere with friends.

However, in another case, family members, perhaps inadvertently, undermined the woman's safety plan by telling police that she was a lesbian, on which statement police became less supportive than they had been – an example of how informal responses may interact with formal interventions, in this case leading to a poor outcome, apparently because of the dismissive, homophobic response from police. Finally, in some cases, the abuser was so violent that the women felt they had to move to shelter or engage police and could not rely only on informal third parties (Kirkwood, 1993).

In a more recent U.S. study of thirty-one women who were in an abusive relationships, no woman was fully satisfied with the informal support she received (Rose et al., 2000). Six women had nobody at all to turn to for support. The other twenty-five received only limited support or for various reasons felt constraint in seeking more support. This was because the family was abusive, because the women were isolated and did not trust others, or because they had suffered such physical violence from the abuser that they were simply unable to seek help.

Two women said that no help came from their partner or the partner's family. If the unhelpful partners were the abusers, this finding seems unsurprising, but it is important because it flags the dilemma that for many women the partner is a central source of economic and emotional support or lends needed respectability and status to women who live in societal contexts that are reluctant or unwilling to grant full personhood to women who are not attached to men. When under such circumstances the partner becomes abusive, women may lose a critical source of multiple forms of support. (In a study with female sexual assault survivors, Ahrens, Cabral, & Abeling [2009] found that most positive support came from friends and counselors, whereas romantic partners provided only moderate support and the highest amount of blame).

Fathers were largely absent as sources of support for their daughters. Many women described their relationship with their father as "stormy" or "cold" (Rose et al., 2000, p. 35); several women had grown up with fathers who were alcoholics, abused drugs, or who themselves perpetrated sexual and physical violence in the family.

Female friends were most often relied on for support, whereas family members, especially parents, were not seen as consistent sources of support. Over half of the women in the sample identified female friends as someone to talk to who would provide emotional support. One-third of the women listed their mother as a person to talk to, and three women listed their sisters. Two women rated their mother's support as 100% helpful and all women rated female friends at least as 50% helpful and in most cases between 75% and 100% helpful (Rose et al., 2000).

RESPONSES IN THE LONGER TERM

Leaving an abusive relationship can be a complex, drawn-out process during which movement toward safety, self-determination, and independence is set back by episodes of danger, loss of hope, and renewed dependence on the abuser. Horton and Johnson (1993) estimated that, on average, leaving takes 8 years. Okun (1986) estimated an average of five attempted separations before women are able to leave permanently. Victims need to establish whether they are able to leave and whether they actually would be better off if they left (Choice & Lamke, 1999). The latter, that leaving means being better off, is often assumed by third parties, even though it is not always true. Among the problems that leaving may not solve is the danger from the abuser, which may continue or escalate (Mahoney, 1991), and the possibility that after leaving women (and possibly children) are homeless.

For informal third parties, the complexities of leaving mean that they may need to have considerable staying power in order to be able to provide support and encouragement over what may be a process of months or years. Hoff (1990) found that an important source of support lay in friends who stood by the survivor for as long as it took her to free herself from the abuse.

Difficulty in trusting potential helpers, often a consequence of abuse, also can make help-seeking more difficult. Through interviews with women in the United Kingdom, Abrahams (2010) found that the disruption of social ties that the abuse had caused required women to rebuild relationships and networks. However, in order to form new relationships with others, the women had to trust them, which they found difficult because of the violation of trust they had experienced in their abusive relationships. This made it particularly difficult to reach out to other people and added to isolation and loneliness.

On the other hand, relatively small gestures from informal third parties, including neighbors, may by enough to help women through particularly vulnerable moments. Abrahams (2010) found that one such moment was the first night women spent alone in their new home after having lived in domestic violence refuges. Although finally being able to live on their own marked an exhilarating achievement, for many women this was also a terrifying moment in which they felt vulnerable to attempts by the abuser to lure them back to him. A visit from a friend or neighbor during this first evening in the new home helped many women navigate this critical passage successfully.

COMPLICATING FACTORS: WOMAN-BLAMING IDEOLOGIES, ISOLATION, AND STRAINED NETWORKS

Disclosure, help-seeking, and informal responses are complicated by a number of contextual factors. Some of them have been mentioned before and are examined again here in relation to help-seeking. These include gender ideologies that deny women the right to decide how they would like to live with male sexual and domestic partners; expressed in rape myths and domestic violence myths, such ideologies blame women for sexual or domestic abuse perpetrated by a male partner. In addition, help-seeking is difficult or impossible when victims are isolated from potential helpers, either by active interference of the perpetrator or through stigma and shame. And finally, help-giving may be particularly difficult for strained social networks, in which abuse is widespread and in which poverty or violence that is due to drugs, gangs, armed conflict, or warfare creates such difficult circumstances that network members may be too exhausted to help or too preoccupied with their own survival.

As discussed in Chapters 2 and 3, gender ideologies shape how informal third parties interpret and assess abuse. The dynamics of rape disclosure and help-seeking are linked to the social construction of rape, in particular rape myths and associated ideas of men's and women's sexuality and what constitutes acceptable sexual conduct for women and men (Horvath & Brown, 2009). Myths about rape and domestic violence are widespread, and their problematic effects on responses to victims are well documented (Bohner et al., 2009). Women's accounts of what family members and friends have said to them in response to disclosure show that such beliefs are held by and influence the response of network members (Hanmer, 2000; Hoff, 1990). Where informal third parties hold gender ideologies that excuse or justify the sexual or domestic abuse of women, they create an environment in which victims risk blame and ostracism from others when they disclose abuse and seek help.

The psychoanalytic work of Herman (1992) and Winnicott (1965) previously mentioned suggests that responses to disclosure are experienced as positive when they contribute to a shared recognition of the victim's dignity and humanity, whereas the denial of the other's humanity constitutes a second injury (Symond, 1980/2010). Misogynist gender ideologies undermine and deny the full humanity of women and, similar to hate speech, contribute to a climate in which the humanity of women is ever so slightly in doubt and recognition of their full personhood is withheld (Wessler & De Andrade, 2006). Where network members endorse misogynist ideologies – be it within the family, at work, in school, or in the community – women face a hostile climate in which disclosure and help-seeking become particularly risky or impossible.

Misogynist gender ideologies can combine with racist attitudes to isolate victims of color even further. For African American women, disclosure of sexual assault is made difficult through racial stereotypes and racialized rape myths (Tillman et al., 2010). A recent study found that both African American women and white women in a U.S. sample received more positive than negative responses from third parties but for African American women negative responses were more strongly related to posttraumatic stress symptoms (Jacques-Tiura et al., 2010). The strong link between negative responses and posttraumatic stress symptoms for African American women may have been due to negative responses from formal service providers and, according to the authors, might reflect distrust in medical and judicial systems.

Pressure on victims not to disclose domestic or sexual violence has been reported from the beginnings of antiviolence movements and in research from all over the world (Andersson et al., 2010; Naved et al., 2006), so that "breaking the silence" has remained an important rallying call in awareness campaigns (European Commission, 2000). Concern about stigma, family honor, or loyalty to one's community may create particular complexities for victims in minority communities (Dasgupta, 2007; Roberts et al., 2010; Thiara et al., 2011; Tillman et al., 2010).

The second complicating factor to be emphasized here is isolation. Isolation of the victim from social support may be a side effect of stigma and secrecy but could also be the result of perpetrators deliberately isolating the victim, and both dynamics – perpetrator-driven isolation and third-party-driven isolation – may mutually reinforce each other (Davies, Lyon, & Monti-Catania, 1998). Fear of retaliation from the perpetrator constitutes another barrier to disclosure and help-seeking (Lutenbacher, Cohen, & Mitzel, 2003). Shelter studies with women who had fled from extremely controlling or violent perpetrators have often found that these perpetrators had isolated their victims from social support by directly preventing women from seeking help, by threatening helpers, or by forcing women to flee to an undisclosed shelter, which for some women may have meant trading any remaining social contacts for the relative safety of shelter. Thus, in this research severe patterns of abuse appear to be important reasons for the increasing loss of informal support victims of intimate terrorists often experience (Levendosky et al., 2004).

Social dynamics that isolate victims may be particularly problematic for women from minority communities. For example, South Asian women in the United States felt that their support-seeking was constrained by multiple factors including cultural attitudes that expect women to be in a relationship with a man and to put up with emotional abuse from a man, along with a sense that their peers and reference groups valued women only in the role of wife or mother and not as autonomous individuals (Abraham, 2000). Bangladeshi women reported stigma and fear of greater harm as barriers to disclosure (Naved et al., 2006). Women in Pakistan reported multiple interrelated barriers including risking their reputation in the community, bringing dishonor to the family, fear of losing their children if the women ended up separating from or divorcing their husbands, and skepticism toward the authorities (Andersson et al., 2010).

Chaudoir and Quinn (2010) argued for a generic approach to disclosure dynamics, proposing a concept of "concealable stigmatized identity" (p. 574). However, research on disclosure in sexual and racial minorities suggests that barriers to disclosure may vary significantly with local circumstances (Dasgupta, 2007; Gill, 2009; Jacques-Tiura et al., 2010; Tillman et al., 2010). Secrecy in itself is a powerful barrier to disclosure as it models silence. In the words of one woman struggling against domestic violence: "No one asked. No one asked me and I just didn't tell" (Lutenbacher et al., 2003 p. 60).

Finally, poverty and violence in the community make help-seeking difficult and put strain on social networks (Goodman et al., 2009). Levendosky et al (2004) compared the social support of abused and nonabused women. This study tried to shed more light on various features of women's social context, focusing on the number of supporters women reported and whether these supporters also were victims of domestic abuse. The authors recruited over 200 women in three mid-Michigan counties at ob–gyn clinics and other sites and by posting flyers in grocery stores and laundromats.

Consistent with other research, Levendosky et al. found that, compared with nonabused women, those suffering from domestic violence had less emotional and practical support (regardless of age, income, or education). However, contrary to a common assumption in the literature, lack of support appeared not to be because abused women were isolated: Abused and nonabused women reported similar numbers of supporters. Nor could lack of support be explained by lack of disclosure: 95% of the abused women revealed the abuse to at least one potential helper and on average mentioned the abuse to 62% of network members (and disclosure, in general, was associated with better emotional and practical support). Severity of violence also was unrelated to support. This seems to contradict findings from shelter studies, but it may simply reflect the fact that here violence was less severe (the authors report as much).

Thus, neither isolation nor lack of disclosure or severity of violence explained the impaired social support reported by abused women. What did explain it? Levendosky et al. found that although abused and nonabused women had similar numbers of potential supporters in their social networks, among the networks of abused women were more members who themselves were victims of domestic violence. At first glance, this might be a good thing because women with similar experiences of abuse might be more understanding because they "have been there" themselves. Nonetheless, some studies have found that similarity of experience (homophily, in sociological terms) can mean poorer, rather than better, social support. Levendosky et al. found that homophily was associated with more disclosure but with less emotional support and more criticism. Thus, victims opened up more to others in their networks with similar experiences, but although disclosure in general was associated with better support, disclosure to similar others was associated with criticism and little emotional support. The authors suggest a number of explanations for this finding. Abused network members may be exhausted to the point that they have few emotional resources left to share, or the negative responses may have been a reflection of depressive symptoms in network members that were brought on by the abuse they were suffering. If this was the case, impaired social support would have been indirectly the result of abuse meted out by other men in the social network. This would imply far-reaching ripple effects of domestically violent perpetrators: primary impacts in terms of direct abuse against wives, girlfriends, or partners, and secondary impacts in terms of compromising the ability of these women to act as helpful third parties to other victims who might also need help.

These findings show how complex the dynamics of informal helping can be. In the U.S. research on sexual assault disclosure, disclosure to female friends was most common and considered most helpful, presumably because female friends are more similar and may have had more similar experiences or outlooks regarding sexual assault than other informal third parties (Ullman, 2010). However, for disclosure of domestic violence, Levendosky et al. (2004) found that disclosure to similar friends (i.e., other women in the social network who were experiencing domestic violence), while common, was *not* helpful, possibly because the very experience of abuse that produced shared understandings also produced exhaustion and depression, both of which may have undermined the friends' abilities to be more supportive.

VIEWS FROM THIRD PARTIES

Few studies have asked network members directly what they think about women, violence, family, and intimate relationships. Hoff interviewed twenty-five members of the social networks of the women in her sample. Of these twenty-five, twenty-two were informal third parties (two were lawyers, one was a pastor). Using a number of value questions, which she asked both the women and their network members, Hoff created an index ranging from 47 to 235; low scores reflected traditional gender values and high scores reflected feminist gender values. The mean score for victims' responses was 186, for female network members 175, and for male network members 170. The numerical midpoint of this index is 141 so all respondents, on average, were in the "feminist" range of the value statements.

However, the overall average conceals complexity within responses: "Most of the network members held traditional views on some points, but their values were quite feminist on other points, with the majority tending more toward feminist than traditional values" (Hoff, 1990, p. 117). More detail about what this meant emerged from a qualitative analysis of the interviews in which the value statements were assessed. This analysis showed that some network members held complex and contradictory attitudes and feelings about the abuse against a family member or friend. Although these findings are based on the answers of only a few respondents, Hoff is quoted here because it is rare to get a glimpse into what informal third parties might be thinking.

Hoff mentions one father who, with a disability pension from work, performed nontraditional routine cooking, cleaning, and childcare tasks at home while also holding traditional values. He and two other fathers

> strongly expressed their disapproval of and helplessness to stop the violence toward their daughters. Two of the fathers spoke of their inclination to beat up the violent husbands if they had a chance. The para-professional father was so exasperated trying to answer people's questions about 'What keeps them together?' that he said 'She must love to be beaten . . . Maybe he's got something on her.' Despite these attitudes, though, he also made

> frequent statements of concern and support for his daughter. A professionally educated father was equally exasperated and frequently blamed himself as well as his daughter. (p. 118)

Thus, informal third parties may struggle with contradictory attitudes toward victims, possibly drawing on sexist beliefs in an attempt to make sense of the abuse.

In a national U.S. sample of 6,010 individuals who had known someone who had been a victim of intimate partner violence during the past year, about half of the respondents, almost 3,000 people, reported that they had done something to help that individual (Beeble et al., 2008). Nearly 90% of helpers said they listened to and talked with the survivor about the abuse. About one-fourth of helpers referred the survivor to an organization or agency, 22% informed a relative, and 18% told the police. Ten percent of helpers offered shelter while the survivor transitioned out of the abusive relationship; 3% referred to a domestic violence shelter. The authors sorted informal responses into three categories: emotional support (listening, talking), formal support (referrals to organizations, agencies, police, church), and instrumental support (offering shelter or financial assistance or helping the survivor escape). Younger third parties were more likely to help than older third parties. Women were more likely to help than men but in absolute percentage points the differences were small, including emotional support, which 90% of women and 86% of men offered.

Latta and Goodman (2011) interviewed two men and sixteen women to whom a friend had disclosed intimate partner violence. Participants were recruited from the Boston metropolitan area and were interviewed on what it was like to have a friend or family member who was in a "difficult relationship." For eleven participants, the survivor was a friend (or friend and co-worker); for seven, it was a family member or in-law. The central theme to emerge from these interviews was network members struggling to define their role: "From the earliest stages of noticing that something might be wrong in the survivor's intimate relationship to choosing to take action, network members asked themselves how best to engage with their friend or family member" (pp. 984–5). This process appeared to unfold in a nonlinear movement among three phases: "becoming aware," "developing a narrative," and "taking action" (p. 985). The shift from being unaware to being aware involved periods of suspecting, uncertainty, and confirmation (a few network members witnessed an abusive episode).

The development of a narrative involved gathering information and making sense of it. Taking action for some participants meant distancing themselves from victim and perpetrator, either by cutting off contact or pretending the abuse was not occurring. For others, taking action meant trying to figure out how to end the abuse. Network members might also switch back and forth between engaging and disengaging. Engaging included naming the abuse, exploring what the survivor wanted to do next, strategic planning, and providing resources. The network members who witnessed an abusive episode physically intervened on behalf of the victim. Some of the network members used their ties to the perpetrator to try and talk to him or provide him resources.

A final example of third-party perspectives returns to the university context. College classrooms, in particular classes in which sexual or domestic abuse are discussed as academic topics, can provide a conducive context for disclosure in which students may tell trusted lecturers about experiences of abuse. Branch, Hayes-Smith, and Richards (2011) interviewed thirty professors and instructors, twenty-three of whom were women, who at some point in their career had a student disclose sexual assault or intimate partner violence. Almost all participants had received multiple disclosures, most of them from current students and in the context of a college course on victimization. Twenty-nine participants had disclosures from female students; one had a disclosure from a male student.

The study examined how professors modified teaching or classroom management strategies in response to disclosures. Some teaching staff tried to create a safe environment for disclosure or encouraged students to disclose in written assignments, whereas other teaching staff tried to discourage disclosure. Overall, responses to disclosure in these teaching contexts were geared toward pedagogy and classroom management (rather than individualized support such as developing a safety plan). Study participants recommended that other professors listen to students and become knowledgeable about local resources for survivors. However, they also recommended that colleges and universities create better support for teaching staff who receive disclosures, including training on how to respond to survivors who disclose and how to debrief others in a confidential manner (Branch et al., 2011).

6

Collusion with Perpetrators

Collusion is used here as shorthand for informal responses that make life easier for the perpetrator regardless of whether third parties intended this to be. Understood in this sense, collusion could include condoning or encouraging the perpetrator's abuse, protecting him from being held accountable, dismissing the seriousness of the abuse, or "staying out of it." The latter may look like a neutral response but whether there is a neutral stance to sexual or domestic violence is debatable; doing nothing may simply give perpetrators the freedom to continue abusing (Bancroft, 2002; Herman, 1992). "Lack of awareness is not innocent, it contains a social value, that of non-intervention" (Hanmer, 2000, p. 15).

To some extent, informal third-party collusion is possible because it concurs with societal frameworks and legacies that have structured heterosexual gender relations to the advantage of male perpetrators of intimate abuse and contribute to "societal collusion and culpability" in sexual and domestic violence (Sullivan, 1997). These societal issues have been discussed elsewhere, including the justification of the violent suppression of women's sexual and domestic autonomy in the name of manliness (Connell & Messerschmidt, 2005; Totten, 2003), fathers' rights

(Dragiewicz, 2008), family honor (Sen, 2005), or husbands' God-given responsibilities (Lundgren, 1998), as well as legal rulings that are lenient toward male perpetrators of sexual or domestic violence against women in intimate relationships while being harsh toward female perpetrators (Jones, 1980; Sen, 2005), and the implications of racism and poverty (Sokoloff & Pratt, 2005; Sullivan, 1997).

This chapter focuses on how informal third parties, deliberately or unwittingly, may enact these gendered frameworks to the advantage of perpetrators. Four patterns are examined: family and friends being co-opted by the perpetrator; family and friends endorsing or enforcing violence against women in their midst; old-boys' networks in which perpetrators benefit from personal ties to agents of the state; and the shielding of perpetrators by superiors in organizational hierarchies.

INFORMAL THIRD PARTIES BEING CO-OPTED: ISOLATION TACTICS, GULLIBILITY, AND FEAR

Case studies provide evidence of how perpetrators try to actively manipulate the social context of their victims (Davies et al., 1998). A common strategy is isolation through which perpetrators try to cut victims off from potential sources of support and that makes it more difficult for victims to get a "reality check" on the brainwashing the perpetrator is doing to them (Pence & Paymar, 1993; Stark, 2007). Women have described in detail how their abuser will prevent them from going out and meeting other people (Davies et al., 1998). In an early study in the United Kingdom, Homer, Leonard, and Taylor (1985) showed how perpetrators of domestic violence cut their victims off from parents and old friends, prevented them from making new friends, and only approved as social contacts the perpetrator's friends who were of no help to the victim. In addition, the abusive men created an atmosphere at home that deterred informal (and formal) visitors. These deliberate isolation strategies were compounded when victims had no parents or siblings in reach or were steeped in values of fatalism and stoicism that prevented them from turning to family for help.

There is less documentation of how a victim's isolation might present from the perspective of informal third parties. There may be different warning signs such as a woman no longer attending, without clear explanation, meetings, or family gatherings she used to attend; no longer inviting people into her home; or being evasive when asked if anything is wrong. If third parties lose patience with the victim or find her stories too distressing, they may retreat or signal that they don't want to be bothered anymore and might end up doing the isolation work for the perpetrator. His "jealous surveillance" (Kelly, 1996) may destroy her relationships with others and others may be afraid that the perpetrator will harm them if they help the victim.

Isolation from informal third parties may present particular challenges to immigrant women, either because they are geographically isolated from family or friends or because family members side with perpetrators and leave women isolated within their families and in the wider community (Menjívar & Salcido, 2002). Another strategy of manipulating the victim's social context is "working" family members, friends, or co-workers so that they act as de facto allies of the perpetrator. Bancroft (2002) describes one case in which an abusive husband whose wife had escaped from him tracked down his wife by charming her parents to give him her address; in another case a woman whose boyfriend sexually assaulted her niece sided with him and attempted (unsuccessfully) to get custody of her niece. (Bancroft also describes several cases in which formal third parties, therapists, and custody evaluators, side with abusive men on the merits of their word, while doubting the victim's word or ignoring evidence of abuse.) Perpetrators can find allies among their own families but also among the victim's (which for the victim might feel like a double betrayal). In one case, a man won over the parents of his ex-wife who were upset with their daughter because she had stopped going to church. He dazzled them with a story about the importance of faith while bad-mouthing his ex-wife as a bad mother and slut (Bancroft, 2002). It may be difficult for third parties to recognize and overcome a tendency "to feel that it is their responsibility to make sure that she realizes *what a good person he really is inside* – in other words, to stay focused on his needs rather than on her own" (Bancroft, 2002, p. 288; emphasis in the original). Twenty years earlier, Lott, Reilly, & Howard (1982) had found that for women who were interviewed about their views of a case in which female students had brought charges of sexual assaults against male students (who all eventually were acquitted) the "dominant (but not unanimous) attitude among those who commented – particularly the students – was greater sympathy for the male defendants than for the female plaintiffs" (p. 317).

FRIENDS OR FAMILY ENDORSING OR ENABLING VIOLENCE AGAINST WOMEN IN THEIR MIDST

Informal third parties sometimes endorse or actively enforce violence against women in their families or social networks. This is illustrated by reference to two lines of inquiry. One concerns research about misogynist reference groups or "abusive peers" – men who condone abuse or are abusive and who are members of the social networks of abusive male college students (DeKeseredy, 1990; Schwartz & DeKeseredy, 1997). The other concerns research about violence against female family members in the name of family honor (Idriss & Abbas, 2010; Welchman & Hossain, 2005).

DeKeseredy (1990) and Schwartz and DeKeseredy (1997) noted that abusive men often socialize with other men who condone or actively encourage the abuse of women. Abusive peers refers to the "presence of *male peer groups* that perpetuate and legitimate the sexual exploitation of women" and articulate and endorse rape-supportive attitudes (Schwartz et al., 2001, p. 628; emphasis in the original). Schwartz et al. (2001) measured abusive peer support by asking men if any of their male friends ever told them to use physical violence or coercion against a girlfriend in order to force sex on her or when she challenged their authority. Men who admitted they had committed rape also indicated that their friends had encouraged physical violence and coercion against a woman. Peer support for physical violence and peer support for coercion each independently doubled the odds of committing sexual violence (Schwartz et al., 2001). Abusive peers can support the perpetration of sexual violence in multiple ways: by rehearsing attitudes that claim men's right to women's sexual compliance, by endorsing and encouraging the use of force against women, and by upholding excuses for sexual coercion.

Silverman and Williamson (1997) found that men who received support for abuse from their abusive peers considered violence against women justified and were more likely to be physically violent to their female partner, consistent with the abusive peer model. The influence of misogynist reference groups was particularly strong when men had little regard for the well-being of others (Williamson & Silverman, 2001). Association with abusive peers may also explain correlations between witnessing violence at home and becoming violent toward women: Undergraduate men who witnessed parental violence were more likely to associate with abusive peers, and these associations predicted men's perpetration of sexual and domestic violence above and beyond the parental effect (Williamson & Silverman, 2001).

Reviewing research on family and peer influences on intimate partner violence, Olsen, Parra, and Bennett (2010) concluded that such influences may start early and combine to form cultures of violence, in which "deviant peer influences" may be mutually reinforcing (Dodge, Dishion, & Lansford, 2006) and in which abuse and abusive attitudes in the family of origin and among friends instill abusive attitudes and abusive behavioral repertoires in boys (Reitzel-Jaffe & Wolfe, 2001). In a prospective study, Capaldi et al. (2001) followed adolescent boys over several years and found that boys who observed their male peers engaging in hostile talk about women were violent against women in their young adulthood.

Abusive peers and the social networks of abusive men are often nested within wider contexts that may have a bearing on abusive practices such as highly competitive or violent environments. For instance, Raghavan and colleagues (2009) observed complex relationships between local context and abusive practices in heterosexual relationships. They found that men exposed to high community violence were more abusive to female partners. In addition, men who had abusive men in their social networks were more abusive to female partners (for white and Asian men more so than for black and Latino men). Finally, men with the highest levels of exposure to community violence and abusive peers reported the highest rates of being violent to female partners.

Studies like these suggest that there may be a higher density of actual perpetrators of sexual violence in some social contexts than in others. This might help to put into context research about the prevalence of potential rapists. For the college context, and simplifying somewhat, the empirical evidence (over three decades of research) supports three somewhat inconsistent conclusions.

One is that a large number (possibly a majority) of male college students are potential perpetrators and would rape if they could (Briere & Malamuth, 1983). The second is that sexual violence is more likely among men who belong to subcultures in which hypersexuality and aggressive sexual pursuit of women are considered desirable (as perhaps in some fraternities and sports teams) (Godenzi, Schwartz, & DeKeseredy, 2001). The third conclusion is that most rapes on campus may be committed by a minority of repeat rapists (Lisak & Miller, 2002).

At first glance, these conclusions contradict each other. However, although they offer answers to the same question (how many rapists are there?), they are not based on the same empirical evidence. For instance, the evidence in the study by Briere and Malamuth (1983) was that men said they would rape if they could, whereas in the study by Lisak and Miller (2002) men said they did rape. As disturbing as the first finding is, we do not know how many of those who said they would rape, if they could, actually did rape. In addition, there is at least a possibility that in the decades between these two studies some social and cultural changes occurred. In the course of the 1980s and 1990s, college campuses have seen a fair amount of antirape education, which may have been successful in changing some male students' attitudes toward rape and consensual sex (but not those who are determined rapists).

Although these particular findings have referred to North American college students, networks of men who share sexist beliefs and endorse the victimization of women – and the subcultures these networks may constitute – are not restricted to adolescents or college campuses. Kraska and Keppler (1995; cited by Schwartz et al., 2001) studied organizational cultures in police departments and found evidence of socially shared endorsement of victimization behavior (from sexual assault to intrusive body searches). Totten (2003) suggested that young male gang members used misogynist attitudes and practices to impress other gang members.

A second pattern of informal third parties endorsing or enabling violence against women in their midst concerns kin involvement in violence against women justified in the name of family honor (Idriss & Abbas, 2010; Welchman & Hossain, 2005). Sen (2005) noted that honor-based crimes "are not solely about individual men controlling the lives of individual women. They are about community norms, social policing and collective decisions and acts of punishment" (p. 48) and include practices of monitoring and policing women's behavior, which are enacted collectively by women and men in the family. Such informal policing includes "constraints on movement, conversations, friendships, choice of marriage partners" (p. 48), but also the murder of women (and sometimes men) for perceived transgressions of honor codes.

The issue of social policing of community norms suggests that family members feel beholden to others in the community. This echoes the notion of interlinking spheres of social influence (Bronfenbrenner, 1979) (see Chapter 3 in this book) in the sense that what matters in the mesosystem of community elders or heads of families has repercussions in the microsystem of fathers, mothers, brothers, and daughters – with the consequence that women pay the price for deals struck elsewhere in the community among elders or family representatives.

Third-party reception of women's protest against rape and domestic violence seems to follow a similar pattern nearly everywhere such efforts take place. Victims and their allies tend to welcome the fact that these problems are finally being talked about, whereas a few vocal elders or community leaders are incensed that, as the cliché goes, their family's or community's dirty laundry is being aired in public. Individuals who try to suppress public debate of these issues may say that speaking out about abuse is a betrayal of family or community (a claim that may be particularly sensitive in racial or ethnic or religious minorities [Dasgupta, 2007; Gill, 2009; Sokoloff and Pratt, 2005] but that historically has been made in white, mainstream communities as well [Haaken, 2010]). Yet, silencing such debates not only betrays victims but supports perpetrators.

OLD-BOYS' NETWORKS: LINKS BETWEEN PERPETRATORS AND AGENTS OF THE STATE

Another form of collusion with perpetrators appears in old-boys networks. This expression is used here as shorthand for the way some men align along shared (perceived or real) interests, which may include friendships or mentoring relationships. The example noted here, strictly speaking, concerns formal rather than informal third parties, but is included because it illustrates the basic issue and serves as a segue to collusion among informal third parties in the workplace.

When studying police responses to domestic violence in a rural part of the United States, Websdale (1998) found relatively strong social ties between perpetrators and police. Local men who beat their wives were friends with the very police officers who should have arrested them for wife-beating. Police officers who should have supported the victim sided with her abuser because he was their buddy. The perpetrator and the law enforcer were connected through social ties and shared patriarchal attitudes. As a result, perpetrators could rely on allies with significant formal power, whereas victims were cut off this very source of power; to them, old-boys' networks rendered the criminal justice system useless.

SHIELDING OF PERPETRATORS BY SUPERIORS IN ORGANIZATIONAL HIERARCHIES

The social context of many perpetrators of sexual and domestic violence against women includes workplaces and educational institutions. These almost always have hierarchical organizational structures in which (mostly, but not always, male) administrators have some power to lean on employees or students to act in accordance with principles of desired conduct. This means that there is opportunity for organizational leadership to address rape and domestic violence (Bell, Moe, & Schweinle, 2002; Kelley & Mullen, 2006). Supervisors, managers, and administrators here are considered among informal third parties because, although they have formal roles within their organizations, they are not formal responders to sexual or domestic violence, neither as victim services providers nor as representatives of the criminal justice system.

From crime victimization data from 1992 to 1996, Warchol (1998) estimated that in the United States each year about 18,000 people were assaulted at work by an intimate partner. Other research estimated that in the United States victimization that is due to domestic violence annually results in nearly 15 million days of lost productivity among employed women and that the annual cost in medical services and lost productivity that is due to injuries women suffer from intimate partner violence is around $5 billion (NCIPC, 2003). Similar findings have been reported from other countries (Walby, 2004b, for the United Kingdom). Domestic violence interferes with women's employment by increasing absenteeism and turnover (Moe & Bell, 2004; Riger, Ahrens, & Blickenstaff, 2000; Swanberg & Logan, 2005). In the United States, women have described a variety of tactics their abuser used to undermine their ability to work, including locking the victim in the house so she could not get to work, beating her before going to work, harassing and stalking the victim, co-workers, and supervisor, making a scene at the workplace, and beating her for actions she took at work (Swanberg & Logan, 2005).

How do third parties in the workplace respond to domestic violence? A corporate survey in the early 1990s found that many employers were aware that domestic violence affected their bottom line, but nearly all of them felt that addressing domestic violence was the responsibility of domestic violence projects in the community (Roper Starch Worldwide for Liz Claiborne, 1994). In 1992, Stanley found that only 20% of victims received any help from employers, most of it value laden and simplistic (cited in Swanberg, Logan, & Macke, 2006). Since then – through policies and employee training – workplace support for victims has improved (NIOSH, 2006; Swanberg et al., 2006). Swanberg and Logan (2005) found that although only half of the women who were victims of domestic violence told anybody at work, of those who did tell supervisors or managers, over 80% felt they received some sort of support such as feeling backed up and understood, having somebody else screen phone calls, arranging more flexible work hours, and having the abuser escorted off the premises.

Of particular interest here are workplace practices through which employers have sided with perpetrators. In a study in Maine, almost 20% of men who had been arrested for domestic violence said that their employer had bailed them out of jail (Maine Department of Labor/Family Crisis Services, 2004). The employers may have considered these men valuable employees. However, although bailing them out may have made sense for the business, it undermined efforts to hold perpetrators to account. Some employers have fired female employees who were victims of domestic violence, thereby depriving them of an important source of support and indirectly siding with the perpetrator (Swanberg et al., 2006).

Schwartz and DeKeseredy (2008) argued that with respect to crime, "informal social control is more effective than formal social control" (p. 183). It is difficult to determine whether this also is the case for crimes of sexual and domestic violence against women and whether informal social control has been effective here or has failed (would rates of rape and domestic violence be even higher otherwise?). One factor often mentioned in passing that seems to undermine informal prevention of abuse (or at least make it more difficult), is split loyalties in which third parties are attached to both victim and perpetrator.

SPLIT LOYALTIES OR GENDERED HIERARCHIES OF LOYALTIES?

The importance of split loyalties has been noted in regard to children's reluctance to tell on other children (Mishna & Alaggia, 2005). The term split loyalties implies similar attachments or obligations to different parties. However, the research on perpetrator collusion previously reviewed suggests that in many cases of intimate abuse of women by male partners, informal third parties exhibit gendered hierarchies of loyalties, in which they might look favorably on the victim as long as the perpetrator is left alone but in which the victim drops out of favor when the perpetrator is taken to task: "'His mother and I were good friends, but ever since he got arrested for hitting me she won't talk to me, as if *I* were the bad one'" (Bancroft, 2002, p. 277; emphasis in the original; Wilcox, 2006, reports similar findings in a study in the United Kingdom). Perhaps "[n]o one wants to believe that his or her own son or brother is an abusive man" (Bancroft, 2002, p. 277). Similarly, it may be difficult to come to terms with the knowledge that one's friend or valued employee is a rapist or domestic abuser.

There is little public debate on how to grapple with multiple loyalties in a way that acknowledges the significance of social ties and the fear of exposing painful secrets, but that also addresses the injustice inherent in siding with the perpetrator and the need to resolve this conundrum in a way that does justice to victims. Perhaps it is not surprising then when "[family members] oppose abuse in the abstract, but . . . fight fiercely for the abuser when he is their own" (Bancroft, 2002, p. 277). Loyalty to the perpetrator can reach extreme degrees. The family of a man in Maine who had a record of abusing his wife and who eventually killed her and his two children (and then himself) kept blaming the criminal justice system for his crimes, made excuses for the man's gruesome threats to his wife and children, and insisted that he was a good father (despite the fact that he killed his children) (*Bangor Daily News*, June 15, 2011).

Split loyalties also may have deep roots among male friends, not just among family members. Poulin, Dishion, and Hass (1999) suggested that deviant actions can function to initiate and establish friendships among male adolescents. Obviously, friendships can develop without deviancy, but when friendship grows through deviancy, collusion with perpetrators would perhaps be less surprising. Although ostracizing the perpetrator may be one third-party response, this would be less likely (though not impossible) from his friends. In addition, and from the perspective of intervention, it would be important to create public debate on split loyalties and learning how to challenge a friend's abuse rather than colluding with it by ostensibly "staying out of it." This also means that discourses about healthy relationships, so far articulated mostly in reference to the micro-system of intimate heterosexual relationships, might benefit from addressing the social construction of respectful gender relations in the meso-system of same-sex male friendships.

Loyalties seem to reflect specific constructions of what it means to be a good family member or friend. These become problematic when goodness is equated with unconditional approval and lack of criticism. The idea that somebody will stick with us through thick and thin has allure, but actually doing so on behalf of rapists and abusers comes at a price. However, if the goodness of close ties was understood differently, split loyalties might have significant potential for the prevention of abuse. In contexts in which learning, growth, and innovation are considered central values (and contexts in which change is welcomed, such as in teaching and innovation), unconditional approval of problematic actions would be considered counterproductive, whereas constructive criticism would be a sign of appreciation and concern. Family relationships and friendships also benefit from learning and growth and, in theory at least, there is potential in split loyalties because they constitute conduits of influence. Using them requires some rethinking of traditional notions of loyalty so that it becomes possible to be a better friend to him by standing up for his wife or girlfriend.

Finally, split loyalties may be less about loyalty than fear. In a study by Carlson (2008), young college men articulated a striking gap between, on one hand, evoking men's need to not appear weak in front of other men and, on the other hand, reluctance to demonstrate strength when there was an opportunity to do so. This gap appeared in conversations about three hypothetical scenarios in which men were violent to another person. In one scenario, two men are beating up a third man, while other people look on. In the second scenario, a man is shoving around a girl who pleads with him to stop, while other people look on. In the third scenario, a man is raping a woman, while other men stand around, seemingly waiting for their turn to rape her. In each scenario the simple ethical response would be to help the victim, and in each scenario this is scary because the perpetrators or onlookers might attack or become nasty toward the helper. Thus, these would be prime opportunities to not show weakness, and indeed to show courage (i.e., the feat of overcoming one's fears). However, although numerous references to weakness and strength appeared in the men's discussions of these scenarios, the words courage and courageous do not appear at all.

Research suggests that social ties can be used to exert a positive influence on perpetrators. For instance, the bystander initiatives discussed in Chapter 4 try to capitalize on bonds among friends, including men working up the courage to disrupt problematic male bonding. Because this can be difficult, the point is not to leave it up to individual third parties to sort through complicated split loyalties but to engage in public discourses about what it means to be a good friend. Although borrowing from other awareness campaigns can be problematic, the basic idea of such changes in public debate can be illustrated by the U.S. campaign against drunk driving that used the slogan "Friends don't let friends drive drunk." This campaign started out at a point in history at which disrupting drunk drivers was considered uncool and embarrassing, but such attitudes have changed dramatically. Similarly, social norming and bystander campaigns try to create a context in which the meaning of gendered loyalties can be reconsidered so that victim-supportive practices become more likely.

7

Summary and Conclusions

The research discussed in the preceding chapters illustrates the scope and diversity of informal responses to sexual and domestic violence against women, their impacts on victims and perpetrators, and their role in maintaining societies free from such abuses. Although informal third parties play a significant role in supporting victims and ameliorating the impact of violence, they can also play into the hands of perpetrators. This can happen in different ways. Informal third parties may blame victims or deny them support, exonerate perpetrators, or help them escape sanctions. Through these different responses and their concurrent effects on victims and perpetrators, informal third parties shape the social context of sexual and domestic violence and the dynamics of risk and opportunity in which victims and perpetrators operate.

Informal third parties are often the first port of call and may act as gatekeepers to other resources. Informal responses are critical because they wield considerable influence over the trajectory of healing and recovery: Positive responses tend to empower victims and may help the victims gain further support if needed, whereas negative responses can entrap victims in shame, blame, and isolation. Informal responses also send strong signals to perpetrators about whether their abuse is accepted or whether it will not be tolerated. Informal third parties can shape access to symbolic and material resources, and their responses to either victim or perpetrator can have simultaneous implications for both. Family and friendship ties link victims, perpetrators, and third parties within complex social ecologies, in which interactions in mesosystems can affect the balance of power between victim and perpetrator.

The boundary between informal response and formal intervention may not always be clear-cut, and can vary across space and time. When formal interventions are out of reach, informal responses constitute *the* societal response to abuse. Where formal interventions are well developed and accessible, informal responses often have important gate-keeping functions. Wilcox (2006) found that for several of her respondents mothers and female friends encouraged the victim to go to the police or seek legal or medical help. Whether social network members are the only third parties involved or whether they act as links to formal services, it is important to gain a better understanding of how informal responses and formal services coexist and how they could be coordinated better toward more effective prevention.

The distinction between formal interventions on the one hand and informal responses on the other stems from countries where a formal sector of specialized victim support, criminal justice, and social service systems exists alongside informal responses from kin and friends (Kelly, 1996). The extent to which formal sectors exist and are able to address abuses of women varies within and across countries (Coy et al., 2007). Nearly everywhere in the world there seems to be some concurrent layering of traditional gender practices, modern legal systems, religious teachings, local women's movements, and antiviolence activism (Lepowsky, 1993). Informal third parties, like victims and perpetrators, live within these multilayered social contexts. They are not detached from the society around them but rather act within and contribute to local gender ideologies and power structures.

One conundrum in the interplay of informal responses and formal interventions can be illustrated in the struggle of college campuses to encourage disclosure of abuse. Disclosure is an important step in the process of seeking help and redress. Disclosure also allows campus officials to better understand the magnitude and scope of the problem on their campus, respond accordingly, and fulfill legal requirements of crime reporting. In an ideal world, disclosure would be safe, met with understanding and support, and lead to beneficial outcomes for the victim along with appropriate sanctions for the perpetrator. In practice, disclosure is risky, victim-blaming is common, and responses to disclosure may be ineffective, leaving the victim feeling unsupported and the perpetrator unchallenged. Because campus crimes are underreported, the crime statistics colleges are required to compile are poor indicators of actual crime rates, and legal measures enforcing such data collection have been ineffective (Sloan et al., 1997).

Particularly troubling is the possibility that ineffective campus responses may actually deter disclosure and drive talk about sexual and domestic abuse on campus underground. Formal reporting cannot be forced. In contrast, a safe space for confidential disclosure to a trusted third party may be exactly what victims need to sort through the victimization experience, find out which courses of action might be available to them, weigh their advantages and disadvantages, and come to a decision about what to do next (which may or may not include a formal report). Supportive and confidential third-party responses to disclosure may be able to contribute to the safety students may need before filing a formal report.

Women find pathways out of abuse from instances of encouragement and support while dealing with setbacks from blame and collusion with perpetrators. Viewed in isolation, any one informal response may appear of little consequence, but together they contribute to the dynamics of risk and opportunity in which victims suffer secondary injuries or can seek redress and in which perpetrators are held to account or enjoy impunity. Informal third parties can mediate the impact of structural inequality and gender ideologies on women's vulnerability to abusive men in intimate relationships. The social and emotional ties that link victim and perpetrator to their social networks serve as conduits of beliefs, norms, and stereotypes, including rape myths and domestic violence myths; informal responses enact support and sanctions; and sexist practices in other parts of the network may spill over onto the victim.

Three areas of empirical data on informal responses were examined: disrupting assaults, responses to disclosure and help-seeking, and collusion with perpetrators. Their significance was discussed within a conceptual framework in which social ties, gender beliefs, and the construction of personhood form a triad of societal forces through which informal third parties contribute to the social construction of women's ability to decide how they wish to conduct their sexual and domestic relationships with men. This framework is informed by research in egalitarian societies in which informal responses minimize risk and maximize opportunity for women through a number of social practices, including societal acknowledgement of women's full adulthood and public authority and men's willingness to disrupt male hierarchies and resist pressure to achieve high status at the expense of women.

Based on empirical research about informal responses, this book offered an analysis of the practices among family and social network members through which gender and sexuality, interdependence and loyalty, and power and personhood are lived on a daily basis. Abuse occurs within these practices and so do any efforts we may undertake to intervene and prevent it from happening in the first place.

DISRUPTING ASSAULTS: SUMMARY AND CONCLUSIONS

In many cases, third parties are present during episodes of sexual or domestic violence against women. These are not always private crimes without witnesses. Many more people have witnessed such episodes than are recognized. This includes children who live in households in which their father or another man abuses their mother. Although the presence of children has been viewed primarily as an issue of their exposure to domestic violence and the trauma that may result, they frequently come to their mother's aid and thus play an important role as active bystanders. The policy response to this has been problematic. In some cases, abused mothers, rather than perpetrators, have been held legally responsible for exposing their children to abuse.

College parties are another context in which informal third parties may witness abuse in progress. Sexual violence against female students is relatively common. Rape-prevention programming at higher education institutions in North America recently has seen a surge in interest in so-called bystander programs. These teach students how to recognize signs that a perpetrator is building up to a sexual assault and how to disrupt this process, either by distracting the perpetrator or protecting the victim. Evaluations of these programs show promising results in terms of participants' self-reported attitudes and behaviors. It remains to be seen whether bystander training increases actual bystander intervention should the need arise and whether that contributes to a decrease in victimization rates.

Taken together, this research suggests that informal disruption in some contexts (e.g., children's interventions in domestic violence) is perhaps more common that one might think and that in others (e.g., student intervention in sexual assault at college parties) the ability to preempt assault could be systematically developed. The evidence also shows that the circumstances in which informal third parties intervene vary considerably with the age of the participants, the relationship to victim and perpetrator, and the setting of the assault. Domestic and sexual violence are not a singular phenomenon and neither is interference in abusive episodes. Informal disruption is varied and complex, posing numerous challenges to research and policy. Although informal third parties may be traumatized by witnessing abuse and may intervene at own risk, it is clear that they do intervene and that they often intervene with success. There also is reason to believe that the potential of bystanders to intervene effectively has not yet been fully realized and that appropriate campaigns or training programs may be able to realize this potential.

RESPONSES TO DISCLOSURE AND HELP-SEEKING: SUMMARY AND CONCLUSIONS

Most of the current research on responses to disclosure has emphasized individual outcomes, focusing on the positive and negative impacts on victims' health and outlook. In addition, there is a social and structural dimension to responses to disclosure in the sense that they contribute to an environment in families, communities, and organizations that is more or less conducive to disclosure. Thus, responses to disclosure create (and fail to create) opportunities for healing, recovery, and redress on individual, social, and institutional levels.

Negative responses to disclosure and help-seeking include doubt, dismissal, ridicule, or victim-blaming, whereas positive responses include listening, consoling, offering help, and providing space to articulate difficult experiences. Informal third parties also offer advice and provide practical help. The latter may include shelter, money, or childcare, rescue missions to help a victim escape from the residence she shares with the perpetrator, or, occasionally, attacks against the perpetrator.

However, third parties also contribute to barriers that keep victims from disclosing or seeking help in the first place. Barriers often involve atmospheres of secrecy in which nobody asks and nobody tells, the stigma attached to sexual or domestic violence, the silencing of "bad news" about the family or the community, and fear of retaliation from the perpetrator or his allies. These barriers can be intertwined, for instance, when secrecy and stigma are backed up by threats of punishment for breaking the silence, exposing the perpetrator, or criticizing family or community in public. The decision to disclose is likely to be influenced by the survivor's assessment of the specific social and cultural context in which the disclosure would occur. This may be complicated further when victim-blame is internalized and when violence is so normalized that it is considered a taken-for-granted aspect of gender relations.

Under supportive conditions, disclosure and help-seeking may be empowering, for instance, when victims can voice experiences that have been silenced and through which they may be able to promote healing and collective action against abuse. For this to happen, however, there needs to be a supportive response from third parties and an atmosphere in which the victim can expect help and solidarity. When this is not forthcoming or when victims expect to be met with blame, ridicule, or further abuse, disclosure is unlikely or may lead to further trauma and marginalization (Ullman, 2010).

Many social practices produce complicated and ambivalent positions for women when they marry or enter into sexual relationships with men. These positions emerge from gendered power relations intertwined with social and cultural expectations of men's entitlement to women and women's obligations toward members of their new family and their family of origin (Baumgartner, 1993; Brown, 1999). These factors may undermine effective support from family members and in particular the development of solidarity among women in the family. For instance, relationships between young wives and their mothers-in-law can be particularly difficult in contexts in which women count for little until they have produced sons. This may result in strong alliances between mothers and adult sons against sons' wives, which in turn can isolate the next generation of daughters-in-law (Brown, 1999).

COLLUSION WITH PERPETRATORS: SUMMARY AND CONCLUSIONS

Informal third parties become brokers of social influence and institutional power by offering or denying symbolic and material assets to victims and perpetrators. Symbolic assets include prestige and respect. An example of conferring prestige on perpetrators of sexual violence is to invoke rape myths that bad-mouth victims and exonerate perpetrators (Horvath & Brown, 2009). Material assets include financial resources and legal or other social services. Access to these is to a considerable extent through networks of social ties (family wealth, "old-boys" networks, alumni networks, having served in the military together, and other ways of "having connections"). Through such links, social networks straddle private and public spheres and informal third parties become brokers of social influence and institutional power. In principle, such influence could work similarly on behalf of women and men. In practice, there is a considerable gender gap in wealth and in links to institutional power (Connell, 2005). References to family wealth and political connections do not mean that all perpetrators are privileged and all victims are desolate. It is a matter of relative advantage and disadvantage, of relative risk and relative opportunity, and in this regard, when viewed worldwide and at a population level, various practices persist that tip the balance of risk and opportunity against (mostly female) victims and in favor of (mostly male) perpetrators.

Historical accounts suggest that collusion with domestically violent men is nothing new (Pleck, 2004). However, Bancroft suspects that as formal interventions become more supportive of women dealing with abusive men (as in better victim support and police response, prosecution and sentencing – not everywhere and not always but better than before the mid-1970s women's movements), seeking informal allies may become even more important for perpetrators who may experience pushback from formal systems. If this was the case, informal collusion with perpetrators would be even more significant, both as a problem and as an area for social change.

SOCIAL CHANGE

This book argued that informal responses contribute to the social construction of women's relative autonomy in their sexual and domestic relationships with men. The empirical data on informal responses suggest how third parties can support this autonomy through the acknowledgement – at interpersonal, family, and community levels – of women's full personhood. Where this is done, as seems to be the case in a few indigenous societies, sexual and domestic abuse are rare. In the societies referenced in Chapter 2, egalitarian gender relations seemed to go hand in hand with considerate, nonviolent heterosexual relationships. More specifically, such nonviolence appeared to emerge from social practices through which third parties realized egalitarian power relations and a general ethos of peacefulness, tolerance, and respect for everyone in the community (Lepowsky, 1993; Mitchell, 1999). Thus, sexual and domestic abuse of women are likely to be absent or rare where gender equality and women's full personhood are *realized* at *all* levels of society, from the microsystems of intimate relationships to the mesosystems of social networks and the macrosystems of societal governance. Where they are not yet realized but are still in a process of transformation, or where they are not realized at all levels of society, the struggle continues. Indeed, the very efforts to prevent abuse may temporarily encounter backlash and the risk of escalated abuse.

In an analysis of U.S. states, Yllö (1983) reported that wife-beating was least frequent where women's status was at "midrange," most frequent where women's status was lowest, and somewhat frequent where women's status was highest. This latter finding led to a "backlash" interpretation of male violence against female partners: When women's status rises above some men's comfort levels, the men may use more violence to keep women in place (see Bridges-Whaley & Messner, 2002, for an extension of this argument to intimate homicides of women). The unfolding of risk when trying to rebalance severe gender inequality and lack of regard for women is particularly obvious in cases in which men stalked, terrorized, raped, or otherwise abused wives or female partners who tried to leave them (DeKeseredy & Schwartz, 2008; Mahoney, 1991).

Furthermore, when gender equality is realized only in some regards but not across societal practices, it may have little to no impact on sexual or domestic abuse (Michalos, 2000). Cross-cultural comparisons have revealed the complexity and layering of social practices and ideologies, often with contradictory results for victims' ability to seek redress, safety, and acknowledgment.

Women's social status is a multifaceted phenomenon. Protective effects of gender equality in law and employment do not automatically translate into lives free from intimate abuse. In the former East Germany, for instance, women enjoyed considerable legal, educational, and economic equality with men, but within intimate relationships practices of heterosexual inequality continued and sexual and domestic violence against women were significant problems (Schröttle, 1999). It is not enough to have laws against discrimination and abuse on the books; they also need to be enforced and, even more important, the spirit of such laws needs to be lived in daily practice – a task that falls to informal and formal third parties (Merry, 2005).

Kelly (1996) had argued that in the long run, "women's kinship and friendship networks, their neighborhoods and workplaces . . . may prove to be a key resource not only in establishing safety for women and children, but also in beginning to decrease the prevalence" of violence against women (p. 67). This positive potential of social networks needs to be set against the negative potential visible in the evidence on abusive peers and collusion with perpetrators (Schwartz & DeKeseredy, 1997). The latter suggests that network members can directly or indirectly endanger women and contribute to the continuation of abuse. Some third parties are supportive and can be trusted but others are not.

Assumptions that "the family" or "the community" are always best suited to address sexual and domestic violence in their midst are problematic. Families and communities are diverse social entities, affected by sexism, racism, and homophobia and by understandings of gender relations that often shift the dynamic of risk and opportunity in favor of perpetrators. Where support is not available, those who try to build safety may need to "create *substitute* sources of social support" (Hoff, 1990, p. 83, emphasis in the original). The task of lowering risk for victims and raising the bar for perpetrators is a communal task but not one to be left to a community defined in perpetrator-friendly terms.

Although network members are often close to victims and perpetrators, they are not automatically well equipped to deal with abuse. Misconceptions about the dynamics of abuse and its consequences for victims are widespread; split loyalties within families and social networks often complicate taking action; in many cases effective action against perpetrators or on behalf of victims requires more resources than informal third parties have at their disposal.

Nonetheless, informal responses are essential. For one, formal interventions come into play only in a minority of cases; in all others, informal responses are it, constituting the social context in which victims attempt to cope with the abuse and in which perpetrators are held accountable or let off the hook. Where specialized victim services are in reach and police are well trained, victims may be able to help themselves without recourse to family, friends, or co-workers but these are still relatively rare circumstances and in the majority of cases informal third parties are the first port of call.

Abusive acts occur within social and interpersonal contexts in which such acts become thinkable and doable for perpetrators and in which victims find it difficult to maintain independence from perpetrators. In regard to sexual and domestic violence against women, this includes contexts in which dismissive attitudes toward women undermine their independence and in which women's autonomy is seen as a threat to masculinity, family, and the social order. Such constructions of gender find their reflection in traditional practices, religious teachings, and legal systems. If and how these are brought to bear on the lives of specific women and men varies across space and time. Whether local practices are conducive to the exploitation of women or whether they resist abuse, among the important sites for this to play out are the families and social networks in which women and men go about their daily lives.

In this sense informal responses in families and social networks constitute the sociocultural bedrock in which abuse becomes possible and in which formal interventions and social change need to take hold. As the capacity of formal services needs to grow so does informal capacity – the ability of informal third parties to create abuse-resistant social contexts. Ending abuse is not only about specialized services delivered by trained professionals. It is perhaps more importantly about 'humdrum' cultural change in which everyone does things a little differently every day.

REFERENCES

Abraham, M. (2000). Isolation as a form of marital violence: The South Asian immigrant experience. *Journal of Social Distress and the Homeless*, 9(3), 221–36.

Abrahams, H. (2010). *Rebuilding Lives After Domestic Violence: Understanding Long-Term Outcomes.* London/Philadelphia: Jessica Kingsley Publishers.

Ahrens, C. E. (2006). Being silenced: The impact of negative social reactions on the disclosure of rape. *American Journal of Community Psychology*, 38, 263–74.

Ahrens, C. E., Cabral, G., & Abeling, S. (2009). Healing or hurtful: Sexual assault survivors' interpretations of social reactions from support providers. *Psychology of Women Quarterly*, 33, 81–94.

Ahrens, C. E. & Campbell, R. (2000). Assisting rape victims as they recover from rape: The impact on friends. *Journal of Interpersonal Violence*, 15(9), 959–86.

Ahrens, C. E., Campbell, R. M., Ternier-Thames, N. K., Wasco, S. M., & Sefl, T. (2007). Deciding whom to tell: Expectations and outcomes of rape survivors' first disclosures. *Psychology of Women Quarterly*, 31, 38–49.

Ahrens, C. E., Rich, M. D., & Ullman, J. B. (2011). Rehearsing for real life: The impact of the InterACT Sexual Assault Prevention Program on self-reported likelihood of engaging in bystander interventions. *Violence Against Women*, 17, 760–76.

Allen, M., Emmers, T., Gebhardt, L. & Giery, M. (2006). Exposure to pornography and acceptance of rape myths. *Journal of Communication*, 45, 5–26.

Allen, N. E., Lehrner, A., Mattison, E., Miles, T., & Russell, A. (2007). Promoting systems change in the health care response to domestic violence. *Journal of Community Psychology*, 35(1), 103–20.

Allen, N. E., Wolf, A. M., Bybee, D. I., & Sullivan, C. M. (2003). Diversity of children's immediate coping responses to witnessing domestic violence. *Journal of Emotional Abuse*, 3, 123–47.

Allen, P. G. (1986). Grandmother of the Sun. In The Sacred Hoop: Recovering the Feminine in American Indian Traditions. Boston: Beacon Press.

Anderson, L. A. & Whiston, S. C. (2005). Sexual assault education programs: A meta-analytic examination of their effectiveness. *Psychology of Women Quarterly*, 29, 374–88.

Andersson, N., Cockcroft, A., Ansari, U., Omer, K., Ansari, N. M., Khan, A. & Chaudhry, U. U. (2010). Barriers to disclosing and reporting violence among women in Pakistan: Findings from a national household survey and focus group discussions. *Journal of Interpersonal Violence*, 25, 1965–85.

Arata, C. M. (1998). To tell or not to tell: Current functioning of child sexual abuse survivors who disclosed their victimization. *Child Maltreatment*, 3(1), 63–71.

Armstrong, E. A., Hamilton, L., & Sweeney, B. (2006). Sexual assault on campus: A multilevel, integrative approach to party rape. *Social Problems*, 53, 483–99.

Baird, S. & Jenkins, S. R. (2003). Vicarious traumatization, secondary traumatic stress, and burnout in sexual assault and domestic violence agency staff. *Violence and Victims*, 18(1), 71–86.

Bancroft, L. (2002). *Why Does He Do That? Inside the Minds of Angry and Controlling Men*. New York: Berkley Books.

Bangor Daily News (May 5, 2010). Husson rescuers say God put them in right place. Available at http://bangordailynews.com/2010/05/05/news/bangor/husson-rescuers-say-god-put-them-in-right-place/. [Retrieved 1/17/2012.]

Bangor Daily News (June 15, 2011). Gunman's father says court's denial of visitation rights caused Dexter killings. Available at http://bangordailynews.com/2011/06/15/news/shooters-father-says-courts-denial-of-visitation-rights-caused-dexter-shootings/?ref=relatedBox. [Retrieved 1/23/2012.]

Bangor Daily News (October 5, 2011). Man gets 10 years in prison for knife attack on wife at Husson. Available at http://bangordailynews.com/2011/10/05/news/court/man-gets-10-year-sentence-for-knife-attack-on-his-wife-on-husson-campus/. [Retrieved 1/17/2012.]

Banyard, V. L. (2008). Sexual violence: Current perspectives on prevention and intervention. *Journal of Prevention & Intervention in the Community*, 36(1–2), 1–4.

Banyard, V. L., Moynihan, M. M., Walsh, W. A., Cohn, E. S., & Ward, S. (2010). Friends of survivors: The community impact of unwanted sexual experiences. *Journal of Interpersonal Violence*, 25(2), 242–56.

Banyard, V. L., Plante, E. G., & Moynihan, M. M. (2004). Bystander education: Bringing a broader community perspective to sexual violence prevention. *Journal of Community Psychology*, 32, 61–79.

Baumgartner, M. P. (1993). Violent networks: The origins and management of domestic conflict. In R. B. Felson & J. T. Tedeschi (eds.), *Aggression and Violence* (pp. 209–231). Washington, D.C.: American Psychological Association.

Beeble, M. L., Post, L. A., Bybee, D., & Sullivan, C. M. (2008). Factors related to willingness to help survivors of intimate partner violence. *Journal of Interpersonal Violence*, 23, 1713–29.

Belknap, J., Melton, H. C., Denney, J. T., Fleury-Steiner, R. E., & Sullivan, C. M. (2009). The levels and roles of social and institutional support reported by survivors of intimate partner abuse. *Feminist Criminology*, 4, 377–402.

Bell, M., Moe A., & Schweinle, W. (2002). Partner violence and work: Not just a "domestic issue." *Academy of Management Proceedings & Membership Directory*, SIM C1-C6.

Berkowitz, A. D. (2003). Applications of social norms theory to other health and social justice issues. In H. W. Perkins (ed.), *The Social Norms Approach to Preventing School and College Age Substance Abuse:*

A Handbook for Educators, Counselors, and Clinicians (pp. 259–79). San Francisco, CA: Jossey-Bass.

Binney, V., Harkell, G., & Nixon, J. (1981). *Leaving Violent Men: A Study of Refuges and Housing for Abused Women*. Bristol: Women's Aid Federation England.

Bohner, G., Eyssel, F., Pina, A., Siebler, F., & Viki, G. T. (2009). Rape myth acceptance: Cognitive, affective and behavioural effects of beliefs that blame the victim and exonerate the perpetrator. In M. A. H. Horvath & J. M. Brown (eds.), *Rape: Challenging Contemporary Thinking* (pp. 17–45). Cullompton, England: Willan Publishing.

Bohner, G., Jarvis, C., Eyssel, F., & Siebler, F. (2005). The causal impact of rape myth acceptance on men's rape proclivity: Comparing sexually coercive and non-coercive men. *European Journal of Social Psychology*, 35, 819–28.

Bonta, B. D. (1997). Cooperation and competition in peaceful societies. *Psychological Bulletin*, 121, 299–320.

Borja, S. E., Callahan, J. L., & Long, P. J. (2006). Positive and negative adjustment and social support of sexual assault survivors. *Journal of Traumatic Stress*, 19, 905–14.

Bornstein, D. R., Fawcett, J., Sullivan, M., Senturia, K. D., & Shiu-Thornton, S. (2006). Understanding the experiences of lesbian, bisexual, and trans survivors of domestic violence: A qualitative study. *Journal of Homosexuality*, 51, 159–81.

Bottoms, B. L., Rudnicki, A. G., & Epstein, M. E. (2007). A retrospective study of factors affecting the disclosure of childhood sexual and physical abuse. In M.-E. Pipe, M. Lamb., Y. Orbach, & A.-C. Cedarborg (eds.), *Child Sexual Abuse: Disclosure, Delay, and Denial* (pp. 175–94). Mahwah, NJ: Erlbaum.

Bowker, L. H. (1983). *Beating Wife-Beating*. Lexington, MA: Lexington Books.

Branch, K. A., Hayes-Smith, R., & Richards, T. N. (2011). Professors' experiences with student disclosures of sexual assault and intimate partner violence: How "helping" students can inform teaching practices. *Feminist Criminology*, 6(1), 54–75.

Bridges-Whaley, R. & Messner, S. F. (2002). Gender equality and gendered homicides. *Homicide Studies: An Interdisciplinary & International Journal*, 6, 188–210.

Briere, J. & Malamuth, N. M. (1983). Self-reported likelihood of sexually aggressive behavior: Attitudinal versus sexual explanations. *Journal of Research in Personality*, 17, 315–23.

Bronfenbrenner, U. (1979). *The Ecology of Human Development: Experiments by Nature and Design*. Cambridge, MA: Harvard University Press.

Brown, A. L. (2010). Personal and perceived peer attitudes supporting sexual aggression as predictors of male college students' willingness to intervene against sexual aggression. *Journal of Interpersonal Violence*, 25(3), 503–17.

Brown, J. K. (1999). Introduction: Definitions, assumptions, themes, and issues. In D. A. Counts, J. K. Brown, & J. C. Campbell (eds.), *To Have and To Hit: Cultural Perspectives on Wife Beating* (pp. 3–26). Urbana, IL: University of Illinois Press.

Buchwald, E., Fletcher, P., & Roth, M. (2005). *Transforming a Rape Culture* (revised edition). Minneapolis, MN: Milkweed Editions.

Budde, S. & Scheune, P. (2004). Informal social support interventions and their role in violence prevention: An agenda for future evaluation. *Journal of Interpersonal Violence*, 19, 341–55.

Burn, S. M. (2009). A situational model of sexual assault prevention through bystander intervention. *Sex Roles*, 60, 779–92.

Burt, M. R. (1980). Cultural myths and support for rape. *Journal of Personality and Social Psychology*, 38, 217–30.

Campbell, R. M., Sefl, T., Barnes, H. E., Ahrens, C. E., Wasco, S. M., & Zaragoza-Diesfeld, Y. (1999). Community services for rape survivors: Enhancing psychological well-being or increasing trauma? *Journal of Consulting and Clinical Psychology*, 67, 847–58.

Capaldi, D. M., Dishion, T. J., Stoolmiller, M., & Yoerger, K. (2001). Aggression toward female partners by at-risk young men: The contribution of male adolescent friendships. *Developmental Psychology*, 37, 61–73.

Carlson, M. (2008). I'd rather go along and be considered a man: Masculinity and bystander intervention. *Journal of Men's Studies*, 16, 3–17.

Casey, E. A. & Beadnell, B. (2010). The structure of male adolescent peer networks and risk for intimate partner violence perpetration: Findings from a national sample. *Journal of Youth and Adolescence*, 39, 620–33.

Chaudoir, S. R. & Quinn, D. M. (2010). Revealing concealable stigmatized identities: The impact of disclosure motivations and positive first-disclosure experiences on fear of disclosure and well-being. *Journal of Social Issues*, 66(3), 570–84.

Chen, Y. & Ullman, S. E. (2010). Women's reporting of sexual and physical violence assaults to police in the National Violence Against Women survey. *Violence Against Women*, 16(3), 262–79.

Choice, P. & Lamke, L. K. (1999). Stay/leave decision-making processes in abusive dating relationships. *Personal Relationships*, 6, 351–67.

Clay-Warner, J., & Burt, C. H. (2005). Rape reporting after reforms: Have times really changed? *Violence Against Women*, 11, 150–76.

Coker, A. L., Cook-Craig, P. G., Williams, C. M., Fisher, B. S., Clear, E. R., Garcia, L. S., & Hegge, L. M. (2011). Evaluation of Green Dot: An active bystander intervention to reduce sexual violence on college campuses. *Violence Against Women*, 17(6), 777–96.

Connell, R. (2006). Glass ceilings or gendered institutions? Mapping the gender regimes of public sector worksites. *Public Administration Review*, 66, 837–49.

Connell, R. W. (2005). *Masculinities* (2nd ed.). Berkeley, CA: University of California Press.

Connell, R. W. & Messerschmidt, J. W. (2005). Hegemonic masculinity: Rethinking the concept. *Gender & Society*, 19, 829–59.

Counts, D. A., Brown, J. K., & Campbell, J. C. (eds.) (1999). *To Have and To Hit: Cultural Perspectives on Wife-Beating*. Urbana/Chicago: University of Illinois Press.

Coy, M., Kelly, L., & Foord, J. (2007). *Map of Gaps: The Postcode Lottery of Violence Against Women Support Services in Britain*. London: End Violence Against Women Coalition/Equality and Human Rights Commission.

Crenshaw, K. W. (1991). Mapping the margins: Intersectionality, identity politics, and violence against women of color. *Stanford Law Review*, 43, 1241–99.

Dasgupta, S. D. (ed.) (2007). *Body Evidence: Intimate Violence Against South Asian Women in America*. New Brunswick, NJ: Rutgers University Press.

Davies, J. M., Lyon, E., & Monti-Catania, D. (1998). *Safety Planning With Battered Women: Complex Lives/Difficult Choices.* Thousand Oaks, CA: Sage.

Deer, S. (2004). Toward an indigenous jurisprudence of rape. *Kansas Journal of Law and Public Policy*, 14, 121–54.

DeKeseredy, W. S. (1990). Woman abuse in dating relationships: The contribution of male peer support. *Sociological Inquiry*, 60, 236–43.

DeKeseredy, W. S. & Kelly, K. (1993). The incidence and prevalence of woman abuse in Canadian university and college dating relationships. *Canadian Journal of Sociology*, 18, 137–59.

DeKeseredy, W. S. & Schwartz, M. D. (2008). Separation/divorce sexual assault in rural Ohio: Survivors' perceptions. *Journal of Prevention & Intervention in the Community*, 36, 105–19.

Dijkstra, A. G. (2002). Revisiting UNDP's GDI and GEM: Towards an alternative. *Social Indicators Research*, 57, 301–38.

Dobash, R. E., & Dobash, R. (1979). *Violence Against Wives: A Case Against Patriarchy.* New York: Free Press.

Dodge, K. A., Dishion, T. J., & Lansford, J. E. (2006). Deviant peer influences in intervention and public policy for youth. *Social Policy Report*, 22, 3–19.

Donat, P. L. N. & D'Emilio, J. (1992). A feminist redefinition of rape and sexual assault: Historical foundations and change. *Journal of Social Issues*, 48(1), 9–22.

Douglas, H. & Walsh, T. (2010). Mothers, domestic violence, and child protection. *Violence Against Women*, 16, 489–508.

Dragiewicz, M. (2008). Patriarchy reasserted: Fathers' rights and anti-VAWA activism. *Feminist Criminology*, 3, 121–44.

Dunham, K. & Senn, C. Y. (2000). Minimizing negative experiences: Women's disclosure of partner abuse. *Journal of Interpersonal Violence*, 15, 251–61.

Dunn, P. C., Vail-Smith, K., & Knight, S. M. (1999). What date/acquaintance rape victims tell others: A study of college student recipients of disclosure. *Journal of American College Health*, 47, 213–19.

Economist (October 21, 2010). Gender arbitrage in South Korea: Profiting from sexism. Available at http://www.economist.com/node/17311877.

Edleson, J. L., Mbilinyi, L. F., Beeman, S. K., & Hagemeister, A. K. (2003). How children are involved in adult domestic violence: Results from a four-city telephone survey. *Journal of Interpersonal Violence*, 18, 18–32.

Edwards, K. M., Turchik, J. A., Dardis, C. M., Reynolds, N., & Gidycz, C. A. (2011). Rape myths: History, individual and institutional-level presence, and implications for change. *Sex Roles*, 65, 761–73.

Ellsberg, M., Jansen, H. A. F. M., Heise, L., Watts, C. H., & Garcia-Moreno, C. (2008). Intimate partner violence and women's physical and mental health in the WHO multi-country study on women's health and domestic violence: An observational study. *Lancet*, 371(9619), 1165–72.

Eriksson, M. & Hester, M. (2001). Violent men as good-enough fathers? A look at England and Sweden. *Violence Against Women*, 7, 779–98.

European Commission (2000). Breaking the silence: European campaign against domestic violence, Vol. 795. Publications Office of the European Union, Luxembourg.

Everill, J. & Waller, G. (1995). Disclosure of sexual abuse and psychological adjustment in female undergraduates. *Child Abuse & Neglect*, 19, 93–100.

Feldman-Summers, S. & Norris, J. (1984). Differences between rape victims who report and those who do not report to a public agency. *Journal of Applied Social Psychology*, 14, 562–73.

Felson, R. B., Messner, S. F., & Hoskin, A. (1999). The victim-offender relationship and calling police in assaults. *Criminology*, 37, 931–47.

Felson, R. B. & Paré, P.-P. (2005). The reporting of domestic violence and sexual assault by nonstrangers to the police. *Journal of Marriage and Family*, 67, 597–610.

Filipas, H. H., & Ullman, S. E. (2001). Social reactions to sexual assault victims from various support sources. *Violence & Victims*, 16, 673–692.

Fisher, B. S., Cullen, F. T., & Turner, M. G. (2000). *The Sexual Victimization of College Women*. Washington, D.C.: *National Institute of Justice.*

Fisher, B. S., Daigle, L. E., Cullen, F. T., & Turner, M. G. (2003). Reporting sexual victimization to the police and others: Results from a national-level study of college women. *Criminal Justice and Behavior*, 30, 6–38.

Fisher, B. S. & Wilkes, A. R. P. (2003). A tale of two ivory towers: A comparative analysis of victimization rates and risks between university students in the United States and England. *British Journal of Criminology*, 43, 526–45.

Frazier, P. A. & Burnett, J. W. (1994). Immediate coping strategies among rape victims. *Journal of Counseling & Development*, 72, 633–9.

Frye, V. (2007). The informal social control of intimate partner violence against women: Exploring personal attitudes and perceived neighborhood social cohesion. *Journal of Community Psychology*, 35, 1001–18.

Frymer-Kensky, T. S. (1992). *In the Wake of the Goddesses: Women, Culture, and the Biblical Transformation of Pagan Myth.* New York: Free Press.

Fusco, R. A., & Fantuzzo, J. W. (2009). Domestic violence crimes and children: A population-based investigation of direct sensory exposure and the nature of involvement. *Children and Youth Services Review*, 31(2), 249–56.

Garcia, E. & Herrero, J. (2007). Perceived neighborhood social disorder and attitudes toward reporting violence against women. *Journal of Interpersonal Violence*, 22, 737–52.

Gasch, U. (2010). Sexueller Missbrauch in der katholischen Kirche [Sexual abuse in the Catholic church]. *Trauma & Gewalt*, 4(2), 94–104.

George, L. K., Winfield, I., & Blazer, D. G. (1992). Sociocultural factors in sexual assault: Comparison of two representative samples of women. *Journal of Social Issues*, 48, 105–25.

Gerger, H., Kley, H., Bohner, G., & Siebler, F. (2007). The acceptance of modern myths about Sexual Aggression Scale: Development and validation in German and English. *Aggressive Behavior*, 33, 422–40.

Gidycz, C. A., Orchowski, L. M., & Berkowitz, A. D. (2011). Preventing sexual aggression among college men: An evaluation of a social norms and bystander intervention program. *Violence Against Women*, 17, 720–42.

Gill, A. (2009). Narratives of survival: South Asian women's experiences of rape. In M. A. H. Horvath & J. M. Brown (eds.), *Rape: Challenging Contemporary Thinking* (pp. 161–183). Portland, OR: Willan Publishing.

Gillum, T. L. (2009). Improving services to African American survivors of IPV: From the voices of recipients of culturally specific services. *Violence Against Women*, 15, 57–80.

Godenzi, A., Schwartz, M. D., & DeKeseredy, W. S. (2001). Toward an integrated gendered social bond/male peer support theory of university woman abuse. *Critical Criminology*, 10, 1–16.

Golding, J. M., Siege, J. M., Sorenson, S. B., Burnam, M. A., & Stein, J. A. (1989). Social support sources following sexual assault. *Journal of Community Psychology*, 17, 92–107.

Gondolf, E. W., Fisher, E., & McFerron, J. R. (1990). The help-seeking behavior of battered women: An analysis of 6,000 shelter interviews. In E. C. Viano (ed.), *The Victimology Handbook* (pp. 113–27). New York/London: Garland.

Goodkind, J. R., Gillum, T. L., Bybee, D. I., & Sullivan, C. M. (2003). The impact of family and friends' reactions on the well-being of women with abusive partners. *Violence Against Women*, 9, 347–73.

Goodman, L. A., Smyth, K. F., Borges, A. M., & Singer, R. (2009). When crises collide: How intimate partner violence and poverty intersect to shape women's mental health and coping. *Trauma, Violence & Abuse*, 10, 306–29.

Goodmark, L. (2010). Mothers, domestic violence, and child protection: An American legal perspective. *Violence Against Women*, 16, 524–9.

Greenfeld, P. J. (1996). Self, family, and community in White Mountain Apache society. *Ethos*, 24, 491–509.

Haaken, J. (2010). *Hard Knocks: Domestic Violence and the Psychology of Storytelling*. London/New York: Routledge.

Hagemann-White, C. (2003). A comparative examination of gender perspectives on violence. In W. Heitmeyer & J. Hagan (eds.), *International Handbook of Violence Research* (pp. 97–117). Dordrecht, Netherlands: Kluwer.

Hagemann-White, C., Kavemann, B., Kindler., H., Meysen, T., & Puchert, R. (2010). Review of research on factors at play in perpetration. Report prepared for the European Commission. Available at http://ec.europa.eu/justice/funding/daphne3/multi-level_interactive_model/bin/review_of_research.pdf. [Retrieved 3/6/2012.]

Hamby, S. (2008). The path of help-seeking: Perceptions of law enforcement among American Indian victims of sexual assault. *Journal of Prevention & Intervention in the Community*, 36, 89–104.

Hamby, S., Finkelhor, D., Turner, H., & Ormrod, R. (2010). The overlap of witnessing partner violence with child maltreatment and other victimizations in a nationally representative survey of youth. *Child Abuse & Neglect*, 34, 734–41.

Hamilton, B. & Coates, J. (1993). Perceived helpfulness and use of professional services by abused women. *Journal of Family Violence*, 8, 313–24.

Hanmer, J. (2000). Domestic violence and gender relations: Contexts and connections. In J. Hanmer & C. Itzin (eds.), *Home Truths About Domestic Violence: Feminist Influences on Policy and Practice* (pp. 9–23). London/New York: Routledge.

Hanmer, J., Gloor, D., & Meier, H. (2006). Agencies and evaluation of good practice: Domestic violence, rape and sexual assault. Coordination Action on Human Rights Violations/European Commission. University of Osnabrück.

Heise, L. L. (1996). Violence against women: Global organizing for change. In J. L. Edleson & Z. C. Eisikovits (eds.), *Future Interventions with Battered Women and Their Families* (pp. 7–33). Thousand Oaks, CA: Sage.

Herman, J. L. (1992). *Trauma and Recovery*. New York: Basic Books.

Hester, M. (2009). The contradictory legal worlds faced by domestic violence victims. In E. Stark & E. Buzawa (eds.), *Violence Against Women in Families and Relationships: Making and Breaking Connections* (pp. 127–46). New York: Praeger.

Hester, M. (2010). Commentary on "Mothers, domestic Violence, and child protection," by Heather Douglas and Tamara Walsh. *Violence Against Women*, 16, 516–23.

Hester, M. & Westmarland, N. (2005). *Tackling Domestic Violence: Effective Interventions and Approaches*. Development and Statistics Directorate, Home Office, London, UK.

Hoefnagels, C. & Zwikker, M. (2001). The bystander dilemma and child abuse: Extending the Latane and Darley model to domestic violence. *Journal of Applied Social Psychology*, 31, 1158–83.

Hoff, L. A. (1990). *Battered Women as Survivors*. London/New York: Routledge.

Holder, R. (1998). Playing on the football field: Domestic violence, help-seeking, and community development. Paper presented at the Relationship Australia (NSW) 50th Anniversary Conference. Sydney, August, 1998.

Holt, S., Buckley, H., & Whelan, S. (2008). The impact of exposure to domestic violence on children and young people: A review of the literature. *Child Abuse & Neglect*, 32, 797–810.

Homer, M., Leonard, A., & Taylor, P. (1985). Personal relationships: Help and hindrance. In N. Johnson (ed.), *Marital Violence* (pp. 93–108). London/Boston: Routledge & Kegan Paul.

Horton, A. L. & Johnson, B. L. (1993). Profiles and strategies of women who have ended abuse. *Families in Society*, 74, 481–92.

Horvath, M. A. H. & Brown, J. M. (2009). *Rape: Challenging Contemporary Thinking*. Portland, OR: Willan Publishing.

Humphreys, C. (2010). Crossing the great divide: Response to Douglas and Walsh. *Violence Against Women*, 16, 509–15.

Humphreys, C., & Carter, R. (2006). The justice system as an arena for the protection of human rights for women and children experiencing violence and abuse. Coordination Action on Human Rights Violations/European Commission. University of Osnabrück.

Humphreys, C. & Thiara, R. (2003). Mental health and domestic violence: "I call it symptoms of abuse." *British Journal of Social Work*, 33, 209–26.

Hunt, K. L., Martens, P. M., & Belcher, H. M. E. (2011). Risky business: Trauma exposure and rate of posttraumatic stress disorder in African American children and adolescents. *Journal of Traumatic Stress*, 24, 365–69.

Idriss, M. M. & Abbas, T. (2010). *Honour, Violence, Women, and Islam*. New York: Routledge.

Incite! Women of Color Against Violence (2006). *Color of Violence: The Incite! Anthology*. Cambridge, MA: South End Press.

Jacot de Boinod, A. (2006). *The Meaning of Tingo*. New York: Penguin.

Jacques-Tiura, A. J., Tkatch, R., Abbey, A., & Wegner, R. (2010). Disclosure of sexual assault: Characteristics and implications for posttraumatic stress symptoms among African American and Caucasian survivors. *Journal of Trauma & Dissociation*, 11, 174–92.

Jarvis, K. L., Gordon, E. E., & Novaco, R. W. (2005). Psychological distress of mothers and children in domestic violence emergency shelters. *Journal of Family Violence*, 20, 389–402.

Johnson, C. N. E. & Hunter, M. (1997). Vicarious traumatization in counselors working in the New South Wales sexual assault service: An exploratory study. *Work & Stress*, 11, 319–28.

Johnson, M. P. (2008). *A Typology of Domestic Violence: Intimate Terrorism, Violent Resistance, and Situational Couple Violence.* Boston, MA: Northeastern University Press.

Jones, A. (1980). *Women Who Kill.* New York: Holt, Rinehart & Winston.

Kalmuss, D. S. & Straus, M. A. (1982). Wife's marital dependency and wife abuse. *Journal of Marriage & the Family*, 44, 277–86.

Karjane, H. M., Fisher, B. S., & Cullen, F. T. (2005). Sexual assault on campus: What colleges and universities are doing about it. Office of Justice Programs, U.S. Department of Justice, Washington, D.C.

Katz, J., Heisterkamp, H. A., & Fleming, W. M. (2011). The social justice roots of the Mentors in Violence Prevention model and its application in a high school setting. *Violence Against Women*, 17, 684–702.

Kaukinen, C. & DeMaris, A. (2009). Sexual assault and current mental health: The role of help-seeking and police response. *Violence Against Women*, 15, 1331–57.

Kelley, E. & Mullen, J. (2006). Organizational responses to workplace violence. In E. K. Kelloway, J. Barling, & J. J. Hurrell, Jr. (eds.), *Handbook of Workplace Violence* (pp. 493–515). Thousand Oaks, CA: Sage.

Kelly, L. (1988). How women define their experiences of violence. In K. Yllö & M. Bograd (eds.), *Feminist Perspectives on Wife Abuse.* Thousand Oaks, CA: Sage.

Kelly, L. (1996). Tensions and possibilities: Enhancing informal responses to domestic violence. In J. L. Edleson & Z. C. Eisikovits (eds.), *Future Interventions With Battered Women and Their Families* (pp. 67–86). Thousand Oaks, CA: Sage.

Kelly, L. & Lovett, J. (2005). What a waste: The case for an integrated violence against women strategy. Women's National Commission, London.

Kilpatrick, D. G., Edmunds, C., & Seymour, A. (1992). *Rape in America: A Report to the Nation.* Charleston, SC: Medical University of South Carolina.

Kilpatrick, D. G., Resnick, H. S., Ruggiero, K. J., Conoscenti, L. M., & McCauley, J. (2007). Drug-facilitated, incapacitated, and forcible rape: A national study. National Institute of Justice, U.S. Department of Justice, Washington, D.C.

Kirkwood, C. (1993). *Leaving Abusive Partners: From the Scars of Survival to the Wisdom of Change.* London: Sage.

Klein, R. & Milardo, R. M. (1993). Third-party influences on the management of personal relationships. In S. Duck (ed.), *Understanding Relationship Processes, Vol. 3: Social Context and Relationships* (pp. 55–77). Newbury Park, CA: Sage.

Klein, R. C. A. (2004). Sickening relationships: Gender-based violence, women's health, and the role of informal third parties. *Journal of Social and Personal Relationships*, 21, 155–71.

Klein, R. C. A. & Milardo, R. M. (2000). The social context of couple conflict: Support and criticism from informal third parties. *Journal of Social and Personal Relationships*, 17, 618–37.

Koss, M. P. & Oros, C. J. (1982). Sexual experiences survey: A research instrument investigating sexual aggression and victimization. *Journal of Consulting and Clinical Psychology*, 50, 455–7.

Koss, M. P., Gidycz, C. A., & Wisniewski, N. (1987). The scope of rape: Incidence and prevalence of sexual aggression and victimization in a national sample of higher education students. *Journal of Consulting and Clinical Psychology*, 55, 162–70.

Kracke, K. & Cohen, E. P. (2009). The Safe Start initiative: Building and disseminating knowledge to support children exposed to violence. In R. Geffner, D. Griffin, & J. Lewis (eds.), *Children Exposed to Violence: Current Issues, Interventions and Research* (pp. 147–66). New York: Routledge.

Krahé, B., Temkin, J., & Bieneck, S. (2007). Schema-driven information processing in judgments about rape. *Applied Cognitive Psychology*, 21, 601–19.

Krahé, B., Temkin, J., Bieneck, S., & Berger, A. (2008). Prospective lawyers' rape stereotypes and schematic decision making about rape cases. *Psychology, Crime, and Law*, 14, 461–79.

Kurlansky, M. (2008). *Non-Violence: The History of a Dangerous Idea.* New York: Random House.

Kwiatkowska, A. (1998). Gender stereotypes and beliefs about family violence in Poland. In R. C. A. Klein (ed.), *Multidisciplinary Perspectives on Family Violence* (pp. 129–52). London/New York: Routledge.

Lakoff, G. & Johnson, M. (2003). *Metaphors We Live By.* Chicago: University of Chicago Press.

Langhinrichsen-Rohling, J., Foubert, J. D., Brasfield, H. M., Hill, B., & Shelley-Tremblay, S. (2011). The Men's Program: Does it impact college men's self-reported bystander efficacy and willingness to intervene? *Violence Against Women*, 17, 743–59.

Latané, B. & Darley, J. M. (1970). *The Unresponsive Bystander: Why Doesn't He Help.* New York: Appleton-Century-Crofts.

Latta, R.E. & Goodman, L.A. (2011). Intervening in partner violence against women: A grounded theory exploration of informal network members' experiences. *Counseling Psychologist*, 39, 973–1023.

Lefkowitz, B. (1997). *Our Guys: The Glen Ridge Rape and the Secret Life of the Perfect Suburb.* Berkeley, CA: University of California Press.

Leone, J. M., Johnson, M. P., & Cohan, C. L. (2007). Victim help seeking: Differences between intimate terrorism and situational couple violence. *Family Relations*, 56, 427–39.

Lepowsky, M. A. (1993). *Fruit of the Motherland: Gender in an Egalitarian Society.* New York: Columbia University Press.

Lerner, J. S. & Tetlock, P. E. (1999). Accounting for the effects of accountability. *Psychological Bulletin*, 125, 255–75.

Letourneau, N., Young, C., Secco, L., Stewart, M., Hughes, J., & Critchley, K. (2011). Supporting mothering: Service providers' perspectives of mothers and young children affected by intimate partner violence. *Research in Nursing & Health*, 34, 192–203.

Levendosky, A. A., Bogat, G. A., Theran, S. A., Trotter, J. S., von Eye, A., & Davidson, W. S. II (2004). The social networks of women experiencing domestic violence. *American Journal of Community Psychology*, 34, 95–109.

Levine, M. & Cassidy, C. (2010). Groups, identities, and bystander behavior: How group processes can be used to promote helping. In

S. Stürmer & M. Snyder (eds.), *The Psychology of Prosocial Behavior: Group Processes, Intergroup Relations, and Helping* (pp. 209–22). Chichester, UK/Malden, MA: Wiley-Blackwell.

Levinson, D. (1989). *Family Violence in Cross-Cultural Perspective.* Newbury Park, CA: Sage.

Lisak, D. & Miller, P. M. (2002). Repeat rape and multiple offending among undetected rapists. *Violence & Victims*, 17, 73–84.

Lisak, D. & Roth, S. (1990). Motives and psychodynamics of self-reported, unincarcerated rapists. *American Journal of Orthopsychiatry*, 60, 268–80.

Lloyd, E. A. (2005). *The Case of the Female Orgasm: Bias in the Science of Evolution.* Cambridge, MA: Harvard University Press.

Lott, B., Reilly, M. E., & Howard, D. R. (1982). Sexual assault and harassment: A campus community case study. *Signs*, 8(2), 296–319.

Lundgren, E. (1998). The hand that strikes and comforts: Gender construction and the tension between body and symbol. In R. E. Dobash & R. Dobash (eds.), *Rethinking Violence Against Women* (pp. 169–98). Thousand Oaks, CA: Sage.

Lutenbacher, M., Cohen, A., & Mitzel, J. (2003). Do we really help? Perspectives of abused women. *Public Health Nursing*, 20, 56–64.

Mahoney, M. R. (1991). Legal images of battered women: Redefining the issue of separation. *Michigan Law Review*, 90, 1–94.

Maine Department of Labor/Family Crisis Services (2004). Impact of domestic violence offenders on occupational safety and health: A pilot study. Available at http://mainegovimages.informe.org/labor/labor_stats/publications/dvreports/domesticoffendersreport.pdf.

Mama, A. (2000). Violence against black women in the home. In J. Hanmer & C. Itzin (eds.), *Home Truths About Domestic Violence: Feminist Influences on Policy and Practice* (pp. 44–56). London/New York: Routledge.

Manning, R., Levine, M., & Collins, A. (2007). The Kitty Genovese murder and the social psychology of helping: The parable of the 38 witnesses. *American Psychologist*, 62, 555–62.

Martin, D. (1981). *Battered Wives.* San Francisco: Volcano Press.

Martinez, M., & Schröttle, M. (2006). State of European research on the prevalence of interpersonal violence and its impact on health and human rights. Coordination Action on Human Rights Violations/European Commission, University of Osnabrück.

Mattingly, M. J. & Bianchi, S. M. (2003). Gender differences in the quantity and quality of free time: The U.S. experience. *Social Forces*, 81, 999–1030.

McGee, C. (2000). Children's and mother's experiences of support and protection following domestic violence. In J. Hanmer & C. Itzen, C. (eds.), *Home Truths About Domestic Violence* (pp. 77–95). London/New York: Routledge.

McGillivray, A. & Comaskey, B. (1999). *Black Eyes All of the Time: Intimate Violence, Aboriginal Women, and the Justice System.* Toronto/Buffalo/London: University of Toronto Press.

McMahon, S. (2010). Rape myth beliefs and bystander attitudes among incoming college students. *Journal of American College Health*, 59(1), 3–11.

Menjívar, C. & Salcido, O. (2002). Immigrant women and domestic violence: Common experiences in different countries. *Gender & Society*, 16, 898–920.

Merry, S. E. (2005). *Human Rights and Gender Violence: Translating International Law Into Local Justice.* Chicago, IL: University of Chicago Press.

Merry, S. E. (2009). *Gender Violence: A Cultural Perspective.* Malden, MA/Oxford: Wiley-Blackwell.

Meyer, S. (2010). Seeking help to protect the children? The influence of children on women's decisions to seek help when experiencing intimate partner violence. *Journal of Family Violence*, 25, 713–25.

Michalos, A. C. (2000). Evaluation of equality policies for the status of women in Canada. *Social Indicators Research*, 49, 241–77.

Michalski, J. H. (2004). Making sociological sense out of trends in intimate partner violence: The social structure of violence against women. *Violence Against Women*, 10, 652–75.

Milardo, R. M. (1988). *Families and Social Networks.* Newbury Park, CA: Sage.

Milardo, R. M. & Wellman, B. (1992). The personal is social. *Journal of Social and Personal Relationships*, 9, 339–42

Mishna, F. & Alaggia, R. (2005). Weighing the risks: A child's decision to disclose peer victimization. *Children & Schools*, 27, 217–26.

Mitchell, W. E. (1999). Why Wape men don't beat their wives: Constraints toward domestic tranquility in a New Guinea Society. In D. A. Counts, J. K. Brown, & J. C. Campbell (eds.), *To Have and To Hit: Cultural Perspectives on Wife Beating* (2nd ed., pp. 100–9). Urbana/Chicago: University of Illinois Press.

Moe, A. M. (2007). Silenced voices and structured survival: Battered women's help-seeking. *Violence Against Women*, 13, 676–99.

Moe, A. M. & Bell, M. P. (2004). Abject economics – The effects of battering and violence on women's work and employability. *Violence Against Women*, 10, 29–55.

Moore, C. J. (2004). *In Other Words*. London/New York: Walker.

Morgan, D. L. (1986). Personal relationships as an interface between social networks and social cognitions. *Journal of Social and Personal Relationships*, 3, 403–22.

Moynihan, M. M., Banyard, V. L., Arnold, J. S., Eckstein, R. P., & Stapleton, J. G. (2011). Sisterhood may be powerful for reducing sexual and intimate partner violence: An evaluation of the Bringing in the Bystander In-Person Program with sorority members. *Violence Against Women*, 17, 703–19.

Mullender, A., Hague, G., Imam, U., Kelly, L., Malos, E., & Regan, L. (2002). *Children's Perspectives on Domestic Violence*. London: Sage.

Narayan, U. (1997). *Dislocating Cultures: Identities, Traditions, and Third World Feminism*. New York/London: Routledge.

Nathanson, C. A. (1991). *Dangerous Passage: The Social Control of Sexuality in Women's Adolescence*. Philadelphia, PA: Temple University Press.

National Union of Students (2010). Hidden marks: A study of women students' experiences of harassment, stalking, violence and sexual assault. National Union of Students, Edinburgh.

Naved, R. T., Azim, S., Bhuiya, A., & Persson, L. Å. (2006). Physical violence by husbands: Magnitude, disclosure and help-seeking behavior of women in Bangladesh. *Social Science & Medicine*, 62, 2917–29.

NCIPC (2003). Costs of intimate partner violence against women in the United States. Centers for Disease Control and Prevention, Atlanta, GA.

NIOSH (2006). Workplace violence prevention strategies and research needs. NIOSH, Centers for Disease Control and Prevention, Atlanta, GA.

O'Brien, M., John, R. S., Margolin, G., & Erel, O. (1994). Reliability and diagnostic efficacy of parents' reports regarding children's exposure to marital aggression. *Violence and Victims*, 9, 45–62.

Ohringer, J. & Samuelson, K. W. (2011). Intimate partner violence and the role of masculinity in same-sex relationships. *Traumatology*, 17, 68–74.

Okun, L. (1986). *Woman Abuse: Facts Replacing Myths.* Albany, NY: State University of New York Press.

Olsen, J. P ., Parra, G. R ., & Bennett, S. A. (2010). Predicting violence in romantic relationships during adolescence and emerging adulthood: A critical review of the mechanisms by which familial and peer influences operate. *Clinical Psychology Review*, 30, 411–22.

Opotow, S. (1990). Moral exclusion and injustice: An introduction. *Journal of Social Issues*, 46(1), 1–20.

Organization for Economic Cooperation and Development (OECD) (2009). Social institutions and gender index (SIGI). Available at http://my.genderindex.org/. [Retrieved 3/5/2012.]

Överlien, C. & Hydén, M. (2009). Children's action when experiencing domestic violence. *Childhood – A Global Journal of Child Research*, 16, 479–96.

Paquin, G. W. (1994). A statewide survey of reactions to neighbors' domestic violence. *Journal of Interpersonal Violence*, 9, 493–502.

Pence, E. & Paymar, M. (1993). *Education Groups for Men Who Batter: The Duluth Model.* New York: Springer.

Peters, J. (2008). Measuring myths about domestic violence: Development and initial validation of the Domestic Violence Myth Acceptance Scale. *Journal of Aggression, Maltreatment & Trauma*, 16, 1–21.

Planty, M. (2002). Third-party involvement in violent crime 1993–1999. Bureau of Justice Statistics. Available at http://bjs.ojp.usdoj.gov/content/publ/pdf/tpivc1999.pdf.

Pleck, E. H. (2004). *Domestic Tyranny: The Making of American Social Policy Against Family Violence From Colonial Times to the Present.* Urbana, IL: University of Illinois Press.

Poulin, F., Dishion, T. J., & Haas, E. (1999). The peer influence paradox: Friendship quality and deviancy training within male adolescent friendships. *Merrill-Palmer Quarterly*, 45, 42–61.

Povey, D., Coleman, K., Kaiza, P., & Roe, S. (2009). Homicides, firearm offences, and intimate violence 2007/2008. *Home Office Statistical Bulletin*. Home Office, London.

Potter, S. J. & Banyard, V. L. (2011). Guest editors' introduction. *Violence Against Women*, 17, 679–83.

Prescott, S. & Letko, C. (1977). Battered women: A social psychological perspective. In M. Roy (ed.), *Battered Women* (pp. 72–96). New York: Van Nostrand Reinhold.

Pyles, L. (2006). Toward safety for low-income battered women: Promoting economic justice strategies. *Families in Society*, 87, 63–70.

Raghavan, C., Rajah, V., Gentile, K., Collado, L., & Kavanagh, A. M. (2009). Community violence, social support networks, ethnic group differences, and male perpetration of intimate partner violence. *Journal of Interpersonal Violence*, 24, 1615–32.

Random House College Dictionary (1975). Revised Edition. New York: Random House.

Reed, E., Raj, A., Miller, E., & Silverman, J. G. (2010). Losing the "gender" in gender-based violence: The missteps of research on dating and intimate partner violence. *Violence Against Women*, 16, 348–54.

Reitzel-Jaffe, D. & Wolfe, D. A. (2001). Predictors of relationship abuse among young men. *Journal of Interpersonal Violence*, 16, 99–115.

Rheingold, H. (2000). *They Have a Word for It*. Louisville, KY: Sarabande Books.

Riger, S., Ahrens, C. & Blickenstaff, A. (2000). Measuring interference with employment and education reported by women with abusive partners: Preliminary data. *Violence and Victims*, 15, 161–72.

Roberts, S. T., Watlington, C. G., Nett, S. D., & Batten, S. V. (2010). Sexual trauma disclosure in clinical settings: Addressing diversity. *Journal of Trauma & Dissociation*, 11, 244–59.

Rodgers, K. (1994). Wife assault: The findings of a national survey. *Juristat*, 14(9), 1–21.

Rogoff, B. (2003). *The Cultural Nature of Human Development*. Oxford/New York: Oxford University Press.

Romito, P., Gerin, D., Crisma, M., Scattolin, P., & Vascotto, P. (1997). Violenza fisica e sessuale contro le donne e risposte dei servizi socio-sanitari. Research report for Regione Autonoma Friuli-Venezia Giulia, Trieste, Italy.

Römkens, R. & Mastenbroek, S. (1998). Budding happiness: The relational dynamics of the abuse of girls and young women by their boyfriends. In R. C. A. Klein (ed.), *Multidisciplinary Perspectives on Family Violence* (pp. 58–75). London: Routledge.

Roper Starch Worldwide for Liz Claiborne (1994). Addressing domestic violence: A corporate response. Roper Starch, New York.

Rose, L. E., Campbell, J., & Kub, J. (2000). The role of social support and family relationships in women's responses to battering. *Health Care for Women International*, 21, 27–39.

Rozée, P. D. (1993). Forbidden or forgiven? Rape in cross-cultural perspective. *Psychology of Women Quarterly*, 17, 499–514.

Rozee, P. D. & Koss, M. P. (2001). Rape: A century of resistance. *Psychology of Women Quarterly*, 25, 295–311.

Sanday, P. R. (2007). *Fraternity Gang Rape: Sex, Brotherhood, and Privilege on Campus* (2nd ed.). New York: New York University Press.

Sarkan, N. N. (2010). Childhood sexual abuse and its impact on women's health. *International Medical Journal*, 17, 107–12.

Sault, N. L. (1985). Baptismal sponsorship as a source of power for Zapotec Women in Oaxaca, Mexico. *Journal of Latin American Lore*, 11, 225-43.

Schlegel, A. (1977). Male and female in Hopi thought and action. In A. Schlegel (ed.), *Sexual Stratification: A Cross-Cultural View*. New York: Columbia University Press.

Schlegel, A. (1990). Gender meanings: General and specific. In P. R. Sanday & R. G. Goodenough (eds.), *Beyond the Second Sex: New Directions in the Anthropology of Gender* (pp. 21–42). Philadelphia, PA: University of Pennsylvania Press.

Schröttle, M. (1999). *Politik und Gewalt im Geschlechterverhältnis* [*Politics and Violence in Gender Relations*]. Bielefeld, Germany: Kleine Verlag.

Schwartz, M. D. & DeKeseredy, W. S. (1997). *Sexual Assault on the College Campus: The Role of Male Peer Support.* Thousand Oaks, CA: Sage.

Schwartz, M. D. & DeKeseredy, W. S. (2008). Interpersonal violence against women: The role of men. *Journal of Contemporary Criminal Justice*, 24, 178–85.

Schwartz, M. D., DeKeseredy, W. S., Tait, D. & Shahid, A. (2001). Male peer support and a feminist routine activities theory: Understanding sexual assault on the college campus. *Justice Quarterly*, 18, 623–49.

Sen, P. (2005). 'Crimes of honour', value and meaning. In L. Welchman & S. Hossain (eds.), *"Honour": Crimes, Paradigms, and Violence Against Women* (pp. 42–63). London/New York: Zed Books.

Siegel, J. I., Pyun, L. & Cheon, B. Y. (2010). Multinational firms, labor market discrimination, and the capture of competitive advantage by exploiting the social divide. *Harvard Business School Working Paper*, 11-011.

Silverman, J. G. & Williamson, G. M. (1997). Social ecology and entitlements involved in battering by heterosexual college males: Contributions of family and peers. *Violence and Victims*, 12, 147–64.

Sloan, J. J., Fisher, B. S., & Cullen, F. T. (1997). Assessing the Student-Right-to-Know and Campus Security Act of 1990: An analysis of the victim reporting practices of college and university students. *Crime & Delinquency*, 43, 48–168.

Sloane, C. & Fitzpatrick, K. (2011). Talk about it survey. National Union of Students, Melbourne, Australia.

Smith, K., Coleman, K., Eder S., & Hall, P. (2011). Homicides, firearm offences, and intimate violence 2009/10. Supplementary Vol. 2 to *Crime in England and Wales*. Home Office Statistical Bulletin.

Söchting, I., Fairbrother, N., & Koch, W. J. (2004). Sexual assault of women: Prevention efforts and risk factors. *Violence Against Women*, 10, 73–93.

Sokoloff, N. J. & Pratt, C. (2005). *Domestic Violence at the Margins: Readings on Race, Class, Gender and Culture*. New Brunswick, NJ: Rutgers University Press.

Stark, E. (2007). *Coercive Control: The Entrapment of Women in Personal Life*. New York: Oxford University Press.

Stürmer, S. & Snyder, M. (2010). *The Psychology of Prosocial Behavior: Group Processes, Intergroup Relations, and Helping*. Chichester, UK/Malden, MA: Wiley-Blackwell.

Sullivan, C. M. (1997). Societal collusion and culpability in intimate male violence. In A. P. Cardarelli (ed.), *Violence Between Intimate Partners: Patterns, Causes, and Effects* (pp. 154–64). Boston, MA: Allyn and Bacon.

Sullivan, C. M. (2005). Interventions to address intimate partner violence: The current state of the field. In J. R. Lutzker (ed.), *Preventing Violence: Research and Evidence-Based Intervention Strategies* (pp. 195–212). Atlanta, GA: Centers for Disease Control and Prevention.

Swanberg, J. E. & Logan, T. K. (2005). Domestic violence and employment: A qualitative study. *Journal of Occupational Health Psychology*, 10, 3–17.

Swanberg, J. E., Logan, T. K., & Macke, C. (2006). The consequences of partner violence on employment and the workplace. In E. K. Kelloway, J. Barling, & J. J. Hurrell (eds.), *Handbook of Workplace Violence* (pp. 351–79). Thousand Oaks, CA: Sage.

Symonds, M. (1980/2010). The 'second injury' to victims of violent acts. *American Journal of Psychoanalysis*, 70, 34–41.

Tan, C., Basta, J., Sullivan, C. M., & Davidson, W. S. II (1995). The role of social support in the lives of women exiting domestic violence shelters: An experimental study. *Journal of Interpersonal Violence*, 10, 437–51.

Taylor, S. E. (2007). Social support. In H. S. Friedman & R. C. Silver (eds.), *Foundations of Health Psychology* (pp. 145–71). New York: Oxford University Press.

Taylor, S. E., Wood, J. V., & Lichtman, R. R. (1983). It could be worse: Selective evaluation as a response to victimization. *Journal of Social Issues*, 39(2), 19–40.

Temkin, J. & Krahé, B. (2008). *Sexual Assault and the Justice Gap: A Question of Attitude.* Oxford, UK: Hart.

Thiara, R. K., Condon, S. A., & Schröttle, M. (2011). *Violence Against Women and Ethnicity: Commonalities and Differences Across Europe.* Leverkusen/Opladen, Germany: Barbara Budrich Publishers.

Tillman, S., Bryant-Davis, T., Smith, K., & Marks, A. (2010). Shattering silence: Exploring barriers to disclosure for African American sexual assault survivors. *Trauma, Violence & Abuse*, 11, 59–70.

Totten, M. (2003). Girlfriend abuse as a form of masculinity construction among violent, marginal male youth. *Men & Masculinities*, 6, 70–92.

Tower, M., McMurray, A., Rowe, J., & Wallis, M. (2006). Domestic violence, health and health care: Women's accounts of their experiences. *Contemporary Nurse*, 21, 186–98.

Ullman, S. E. (1996). Correlates and consequences of adult sexual assault disclosure. *Journal of Interpersonal Violence*, 11, 554–71.

Ullman, S. E. (2000). Psychometric characteristics of the Social Reactions Questionnaire: A measure of reactions to sexual assault victims. *Psychology of Women Quarterly*, 24, 257–71.

Ullman, S. E. (2010). *Talking About Sexual Assault: Society's Response to Survivors*. Washington, D.C.: American Psychological Association.

Ullman, S. E., Filipas, H. H., Townsend, S. M., & Starzynski, L. L. (2007). Psychosocial correlates of PTSD symptom severity in sexual assault survivors. *Journal of Traumatic Stress*, 20, 821–31.

Vearnals, S. & Campbell, T. (2001). Male victims of male sexual assault: A review of psychological consequences and treatment. *Sexual and Relationship Therapy*, 16, 279–86.

Vickerman, K. A. & Margolin, G. (2007). Posttraumatic stress in children and adolescents exposed to family violence: II. Treatment. *Professional Psychology: Research and Practice*, 38, 620–8.

Walby, S. (2004a). The European Union and gender equality: Emergent varieties of gender regime. *Social Politics*, 11(1), 4–29.

Walby, S. (2004b). *The Cost of Domestic Violence*. London: DTI.

Warchol, G. (1998). *Workplace Violence, 1992–1996*. Washington, D.C.: OJP, U.S. Department of Justice.

Watson-Franke, M.-B. (2002). A world in which women move freely without fear of men: An anthropological perspective on rape. *Women's Studies International Forum*, 25, 599–606.

Websdale, N. (1998). *Rural Woman Battering and the Justice System: An Ethnography*. Thousand Oaks, CA: Sage.

Weithorn, L. A. (2001). Protecting children from exposure to domestic violence: The use and abuse of child maltreatment. *Hastings Law Journal*, 53, 1–153.

Welchman, L. & Hossain, S. (eds.) (2005). *"Honour": Crimes, Paradigms, and Violence Against Women*. London/New York: Zed.

Wessler, S. L. & De Andrade, L. L. (2006). Slurs, stereotypes, and student interventions: Examining the dynamics, impact, and prevention of harassment in middle and high school. *Journal of Social Issues*, 62, 511–32.

West, A. & Wandrei, M. L. (2002). Intimate partner violence: A model for predicting interventions by informal helpers. *Journal of Interpersonal Violence*, 17, 972–86.

Westbrook, L. (2007). Digital information support for domestic violence victims. *Journal of the American Society for Information Science and Technology*, 58, 420–32.

White, A. M., Strube, M. J., & Fisher, S. (1998). A Black feminist model of rape myth acceptance: Implications for research and antirape advocacy in Black communities. *Psychology of Women Quarterly*, 22, 157–75.

Wieringa, S. E. (1997). Report of the workshop on GDI/GEM indicators. Institute of Social Studies, The Hague, Netherlands.

Wilcox, P. (2006). Surviving domestic violence: Gender, poverty and agency. Houndmills/New York: Palgrave Macmillan.

Williamson, G. M. & Silverman, J. G. (2001). Violence against female partners: Direct and interactive effects of family history, communal orientation, and peer-related variables. *Journal of Social and Personal Relationships*, 18, 535–49.

Winnicott, D. W. (1965). *The Maturational Processes and the Facilitating Environment.* Madison, CT: International Universities Press.

Wood, J. (2001). The normalization of violence in heterosexual romantic relationships: Women's narratives of love and violence. *Journal of Social and Personal Relationships*, 18, 239–61.

Wuest, J. & Merritt-Gray, M. (2008). A theoretical understanding of abusive intimate partner relationships that become non-violent: Shifting the pattern of abusive control. *Journal of Family Violence*, 23, 281–93.

Yllö, K. (1983). Sexual equality and violence against wives in American states. *Journal of Comparative Family Studies*, 14, 67–86.

INDEX